teach yourself®

nazi germany

michael lynch

For over 60 years, more than 40 million people have learnt over 750 subjects the **teach yourself** way, with impressive results.

be where you want to be
with **teach yourself**

For UK order enquiries: please contact Bookpoint Ltd, 130 Milton Park, Abingdon, Oxon OX14 4SB. Telephone: +44 (0) 1235 827720. Fax: +44 (0) 1235 400454. Lines are open 09.00–18.00, Monday to Saturday, with a 24-hour message answering service. Details about our titles and how to order are available at www.teachyourself.co.uk

For USA order enquiries: please contact McGraw-Hill Customer Services, PO Box 545, Blacklick, OH 43004-0545, USA. Telephone: 1-800-722-4726. Fax: 1-614-755-5645.

For Canada order enquiries: please contact McGraw-Hill Ryerson Ltd, 300 Water St, Whitby, Ontario L1N 9B6, Canada. Telephone: 905 430 5000. Fax: 905 430 5020.

Long renowned as the authoritative source for self-guided learning – with more than 40 million copies sold worldwide – the **teach yourself** series includes over 300 titles in the fields of languages, crafts, hobbies, business, computing and education.

British Library Cataloguing in Publication Data: a catalogue record for this title is available from the British Library.

Library of Congress Catalog Card Number: on file.

First published in UK 2004 by Hodder Arnold, 338 Euston Road, London, NW1 3BH.

First published in US 2004 by Contemporary Books, a Division of the McGraw-Hill Companies, 1 Prudential Plaza, 130 East Randolph Street, Chicago, IL 60601 USA.

This edition published 2004.

Typeset by Transet Limited, Coventry, England.
Printed in Great Britain for Hodder Arnold, a division of Hodder Headline, 338 Euston Road, London NW1 3BH, by Cox & Wyman Ltd, Reading, Berkshire.

Hodder Headline's policy is to use papers that are natural, renewable and recyclable products and made from wood grown in sustainable forests. The logging and manufacturing processes are expected to conform to the environmental regulations of the country of origin.

Impression number 10 9 8 7 6 5 4 3 2
Year 2010 2009 2008 2007 2006 2005 2004

contents

introduction: Germany's road to Nazism

This chapter will cover:

- the creation of the German nation
- Germany's defeat in the Great War
- Hitler's early years
- the Weimar Republic
- economic depression
- the rise of the Nazi Party.

Moment of destiny

The psychiatrist at the Pasewalk military hospital in northern Germany found that the majority of the soldiers he treated were malingerers, men who pretended to be ill in order to avoid being sent back to the trenches. But this blinded lance-corporal was different; he was eager to return to the front. This made his condition very puzzling. Despite the blisters from the mustard gas that marked his face, there was nothing physically wrong with his eyes. Yet it was certain from the tests the other doctors had carried out that he could not see. The psychiatrist decided to trick his patient.

'Corporal,' he said firmly, 'I have to tell you that the gas has damaged your eyes beyond recovery.' The soldier slumped in despair.

'Sit up,' shouted the doctor, 'show that you are worthy of being a soldier in the German army, be faithful to the Iron Cross you wear.' The soldier sat up straight.

'The problem is that you have developed cataracts, thick white layers of film that cover your corneas and cannot be removed. You will never see again.' The doctor paused and then added almost as an afterthought. 'Of course miracles can happen. The mind can overcome the body. Will power can produce remarkable effects. But few have such strength of will to overcome their bodily weaknesses... Are you such a man, Corporal? Are you capable of regaining your sight? Ordinary men stay blind, but extraordinary men force themselves to see again. Do you have the strength within yourself to achieve the impossible?'

The ruse worked. Inspired by the doctor's words, over the next seven days the soldier drove himself through an inner sense of purpose to see things: at first, just light as opposed to darkness, then shadows, then shapes, then outlines, then at last totally clear vision. By appealing to the soldier's sense of self-worth, by demanding that he exercise the power of will, the psychiatrist had destroyed the hysteria that had caused the blindness.

This story is more than an uplifting tale of brilliantly applied psychology. It was an episode of momentous historical significance. The year was 1918. The doctor was Edmund Forster, a name largely unknown to history. The cured soldier was a 28-year-old Austrian who had enlisted in the German army. His name was Adolf Hitler.

A few years later Hitler, without going into the details of how he had regained his sight, spoke of his time as a patient at the Pasewalk hospital as the most important episode in his life. He said it was then that he had discovered that his mission was to save Germany and restore it to its place as a great nation. Hitler's recovery from blindness occurred in November 1918, the month in which Germany accepted defeat, so bringing to an end the Great War that had begun in 1914. Thus, by a strange twist of history, Hitler's triumph over himself coincided with the moment of Germany's humiliation. After fours years of bitter fighting during which Germany had lost 2 million men, she had had to accept defeat at the hands of the Allies – France, Britain and the USA.

Hitler was one of many in Germany who believed that November 1918 marked a betrayal of the nation by its leaders. Corrupt politicians at home, not the gallant army in the field, were responsible for Germany's agony. In *Mein Kampf* ('My Struggle'), a book he wrote six years later, he recorded how fierce his feelings of betrayal had been:

> And so it had all come to this. Did all this happen only so that a gang of wretched criminals could lay hands on the fatherland? Hatred grew in me, hatred for those responsible for this deed.

His sense of betrayal was sharper because of the great aspirations Germany had as a nation.

The birth of Germany

Although its culture and language were among the oldest in Europe, Germany was a very young nation. It had become a unified sovereign state only in 1871, and its path to unity had been a remarkable one. Thanks largely to the efforts of Chancellor Otto von Bismarck, Germany was Prussianized. In a series of aggressive wars, backed by brilliant diplomatic manoeuvres, Bismarck led the state of Prussia to victory over Denmark, Austria and France. These successes persuaded all the German states to accept the King of Prussia as the Emperor of a united Germany. The way in which Germany thus came into being as a *Reich* 'empire' under Prussian leadership left it with a powerful military tradition. This showed itself in growing tensions with the two other great imperial nations of Western Europe. Between 1870 and 1914 the new nation of Germany competed with France and Britain for territories overseas. The most notable example of this was the 'scramble for Africa', a rush by the European powers to seize and control large areas of the African continent.

German defeat in the Great War, 1914–18

Imperial rivalry did not make a war between the European states inevitable, but it certainly played a part in preparing for the conflict that came in 1914. The Germans, as did all the peoples of the nations who fought in the Great War of 1914–18, welcomed the outbreak of the struggle with joy and an intense commitment. Now was the opportunity for the German people to prove the greatness of their nation by a mighty victory over their European challengers. Tragically for them, no such victory proved possible. Caught on two fronts, against Russia in the east and France and Britain in the west, Germany had to sustain a bitter war of attrition for four years. It is true that in November 1917 the Eastern Front had closed when Russia stopped fighting following an internal revolution. But on the Western Front the struggle lasted another year before Germany, drained and exhausted at home, agreed to an armistice. The struggle into which the German people had entered with such enthusiasm and confidence had brought them not triumph but disaster.

The powerful feeling of loss that this created was intensified by the terms imposed on Germany by the victors, principally France, Britain, Italy and the USA, under the terms of the Versailles Treaty signed in June 1919.

The main terms of the Versailles Treaty, 1919

- Germany to give up Alsace-Lorraine to France.
- The Rhineland to be demilitarized and placed under Allied occupation.
- Germany to lose West Prussia and Posen to Poland (this was to have the effect of dividing East Prussia from the rest of Germany by the Polish 'corridor').
- Danzig, formerly German, to be made an international city. (The territorial changes in the Versailles Treaty deprived Germany of 4 million people).
- Germany to surrender all its overseas colonies.

- Germany to be deprived of its warships and aircraft and to have its army limited to 100,000.
- Germany to pay reparations, eventually amounting to £6 million.

Nor was it simply a matter of losing territory and paying reparations. What the Germans resented was the manner in which the Paris talks had been conducted. The Versailles Treaty was a *diktat* (a dictated settlement). The German delegation was not allowed to discuss the terms. It was simply told: agree to them or else the occupation of Germany continues and the war goes on. A particularly humiliating clause which the delegation had to accept was one declaring that Germany was totally responsible for the war. This war guilt clause rankled with the Germans ever after and was a grievance that would be cleverly exploited by those Germans who wished to condemn the Versailles settlement and the German politicians who had cravenly signed it.

The impact of Germany's defeat on Adolf Hitler

Yet it was these humiliations that strengthened Hitler's resolve. They changed him from the aimless layabout that he had been for much of his earlier life to someone with a driving sense of purpose. By birth he was an Austrian, a member of a reasonably comfortable middle-class family living in Linz, but he had never shown any great capacity for work. He had thought of becoming a painter and had gone to live in Vienna in the hope of breaking into the art world. But his paintings were mediocre and uninspired and he was not accepted into art college. He had eked out a miserable existence, living in cheap hostels and doss houses. It was this experience that had brought him into contact with some of the poorer Viennese Jews for whom he developed a deep and abiding distaste: 'Wherever I went, I now saw Jews, and the more I saw, the more sharply they set themselves apart in my eyes from the rest of humanity.'

Hitler was still an Austrian citizen when the war broke out in 1914. By a strange chance, a photo taken in Munich captured him as part of the crowd cheering the declaration of war. He immediately signed on as a member of the German army, joining figure 1 map of Germany after the Versailles Treaty, 1919

a Bavarian regiment. As a soldier on the Western Front, he showed conspicuous courage, winning the Iron Cross for bravery as a dispatch runner under fire during the battle at Arras in December 1914. However, his comrades found him distant and detached, someone whom it was difficult to get to know or to like. He found it easier to make friends with dogs than with his fellow soldiers. There was little hint during these years that Hitler had within him extraordinary powers of leadership and oratory.

These gifts perhaps came as a surprise to him also, and it is unlikely he would ever have developed them had the Germany he lived in after 1918 not been so disturbed and unstable. Germany's defeat in the war destroyed the Reich. The Kaiser was forced to abdicate and go into exile. The old imperial government resigned, to be replaced by a republic based at Weimar. From its beginning the Weimar government was a troubled one and never really won the confidence of the German people. This was clear from the series of violent challenges to its existence from both sides of the political divide. Reds (Communists), inspired by the Russian Revolution of 1917 which had resulted in the creation of Bolshevik government under Lenin, tried to achieve a similar revolution in Germany, only to be crushed by the *Freikorps*, a loose organization of soldiers returning from the war who still held strong nationalist feelings and who were not prepared to see Germany fall prey to the Reds.

It was the *Freikorps* who in 1920 backed an attempt by Wolfgang Kapp, a right-wing journalist, to seize Berlin and set up a nationalist government. Kapp's attempt, known as a putsch, failed, largely because the leading generals declined to support it. Weimar survived, but the putsch had shown the strength of German nationalism. It also introduced into German politics a terrifying symbol – the eight-armed cross or swastika, which the putschists wore on their helmets.

The Rise of the National Socialists (Nazis)

It was in the violent atmosphere created by such conflicts that the National Socialist German Workers' Party (shortened to NSDAP or Nazi) came into being in 1919. It was this party that Adolf Hitler, as a minor official working for the Munich local government, was sent to investigate and find out how troublesome it was. However, rather than spy on the NSDAP, Hitler was immediately attracted to its programme, which fitted the extreme nationalist ideas that he had begun to develop.

Key demands in the NSDAP programme, 1920

- The union of all Germans in a greater Germany based on the right of self-determination.
- The revocation of the Versailles Treaty.
- Land and territories to feed the German people and settle its surplus population.
- The restriction of state citizenship to those of German blood.
- Jews to be denied membership of the *Volk* ('the nation').

He joined the young party and very quickly rose to a dominant position. It was now that he discovered his talents for public speaking. Anton Drexler, one of the founders of the NSDAP, remarked 'My god, what a gob he's got. We could use him.' Hitler's rabble-rousing, rhetorical style was perfectly suited to the atmosphere of the Munich beer halls where the party held its meetings. Although Hitler was not himself a drinker, he soon learned how to handle crowds of raucous beer swillers, saying the things they wanted to hear, playing on their prejudices, and leading them to accept his conclusions. There was invariably an aggressive air about the proceedings and Hitler was skilled at picking out and denouncing the scapegoats who had betrayed Germany and now stood in the way of its regeneration.

Violence was not an accidental accompaniment to Nazism; it was central to it. Hitler always represented the Nazi programme as an unceasing struggle, a conflict against the nation's enemies, internal and external. Under him, National Socialism was essentially organized hatred. Its drew its power and inspiration from the desire to destroy. That was why it was necessary to develop a special force to protect the party and Hitler in particular. This was the origin of the SA (*Sturmabteilungen* or 'storm troopers'), a body of brown-shirted thugs whose task was to break up the meetings of rival parties and generally create an atmosphere of menace that made it exceedingly risky for anyone to challenge them openly. Jews and Communists were special SA targets.

It would be wrong to see the German Communists as the good guys simply because they were anti-Nazi. They were just as thuggish as their opponents, as the violent brawls between the two movements showed. It was simply that in Germany the Nazi thugs won and the Communist thugs lost. In nature, like poles repel; it is the same in politics. Nazism and Communism were so alike that they detested each other.

The Munich Putsch, 1923

Such was the support that the Nazis appeared to gain in southern Germany, that in November 1923 Hitler and General Luddendorf, the leading Nazi in the military, attempted to seize power in Munich. From there they planned to march on Berlin in imitation of the Italian fascist leader, Mussolini, who in the previous year had taken over in Italy after a 'march on Rome'. This time, however, Hitler had miscalculated. The Bavarian police stayed loyal to the government and fired on the Nazi marchers, killing some 16 of them and scattering the rest. Although uninjured, Hitler was arrested, brought to trial and sentenced to five years' imprisonment for treason.

As his arrogant behaviour during the trial indicated, he did not regard the putsch as a failure; it had provided the opportunity to spread Nazi propaganda and he vowed that his time would come again. In any case, the authorities were frightened to treat him too severely as his release after less than a year made clear. The putsch quickly became a piece of Nazi folklore, celebrated annually as 'Martyrs Day'.

Hitler's *Mein Kampf* ('My Struggle')

Hitler used his comfortable imprisonment in Landsberg Castle to write *Mein Kampf*, a mixture of autobiography and ideology in which he set out his main political ideas. To the modern eye, the book is a tedious, hysterical rant, but in its time it was held to express the essence of National Socialism: an unshakable belief in Germany's destiny as a great Aryan nation, the rejection of the Versailles Treaty, and a fearsome hatred of Jews and Bolsheviks (Communists). The book was not so much a plan of action as an emotional appeal to the German people to identify their enemies and then follow the Nazis in destroying them.

The influence of the economic depression

Although the Nazis were eventually to come to power in the 1930s, it is important to stress they did not make much headway in the 1920s. Indeed, as Table 1 shows, their early record in the elections to the *Reichstag* 'parliament' was unimpressive.

Nazis	May 1924	Dec 1924	May 1928	Sep 1930	Jul 1932	Nov 1932
Seats	32	14	12	107	230	196
% of vote	6.6	3.0	2.6	18.3	37.4	33.1

table 1 Nazi election performance 1924–32

The basic reason why Nazi fortunes turned at the end of the 1920s was that the party took advantage of the economic difficulties that began to threaten Germany's stability around that time. During the 1920s, the German economy had performed relatively well; once it had recovered from a serious inflation in 1924 it began to make considerable advances in industrial production and the numbers of unemployed workers fell. In addition, Germany enjoyed better relations with its wartime enemies, which allowed it to come to more reasonable terms regarding reparations payments. In such an improved economic climate, extreme political parties like the Nazis, made little progress. Writing in 1930, a German commentator put it in these terms: 'If the sun shines once more on the German economy, Hitler's voters will melt away like snow.'

However, by 1930, Germany had begun began to feel the full blast of the world economic recession that started in the USA and led to a rapid fall in demand for manufactured goods. Producers stopped producing, workers were laid off, shops went out of business through lack of paying customers, and banks collapsed. A general feeling of despair came over the German nation. The Weimar government had no answer. Indeed, the policies adopted by the Chancellor, Heinrich Bruning, merely produced higher unemployment and a greater loss of confidence. It seemed that cruel fate had pushed the nation back to the grim conditions of 1918.

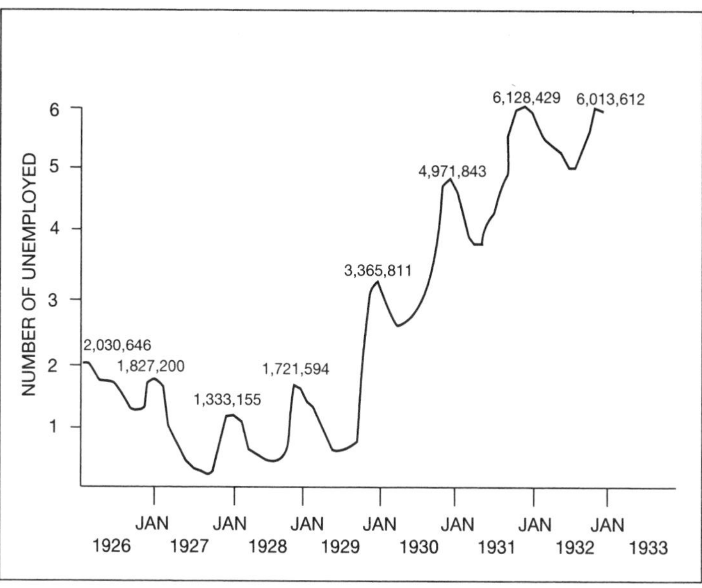

figure 2 graph showing German unemployment figures 1925–33

What saved the Nazis, therefore, from declining into an impotent, fringe party was the state of the German economy. Their popularity serves as a weathervane of the economic conditions in Germany. When things were going well, the vane swung away from the Nazis; when things went badly it swung towards them. Undoubtedly, it was the petite–bourgeoisie (the lower-middle class) who felt most threatened by the economic collapse. Believing that their security and livelihood were at risk, they turned away from the ineffectual Weimar system with its weak political parties and towards the Nazis. This class provided the backbone of Nazi support from now on.

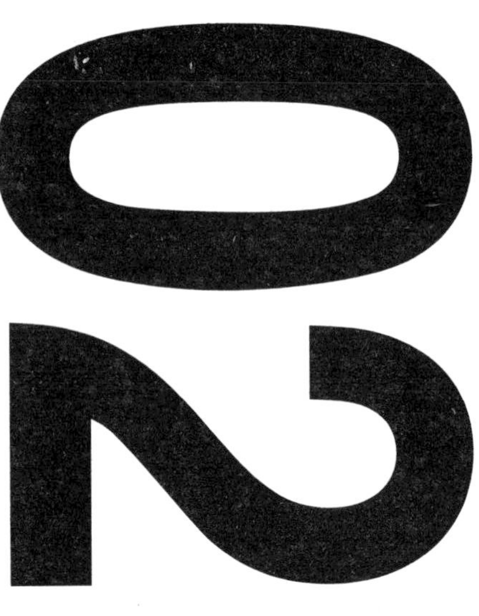

the Nazis take control

This chapter will cover:

- why the Weimar Republic collapsed
- how Hitler came to power
- why Germans voted for him
- how he created levers of power for himself
- how he crushed opposition within his own party.

The end of the Weimar Republic, 1933

At the start of 1933, the Weimar government, after 15 years in office, had little real support in the country. Although the Nazis did not have an overall majority, they were the largest single party. Certainly no other party could match them in their powerful propaganda or in the commitment of their supporters. Whatever the actual figures, the Nazis always gave the impression of being a majority party representing the interests of the German people. That was a consequence of their adept, if brutal, projection of themselves as a party that really mattered. Their skill was in capturing the protest votes of a wide cross-section of the German people. The Communist threat, the Jewish menace to the Aryan race, unemployment, the injustice of the Versailles settlement, the uncertainties of the financial and economic situation that threatened to wipe out the livelihood of the people: these were the fears the Nazis played upon to attract the leading industrials and persuade the middle classes to accept their cause.

Hitler's ability to appeal across the range of classes had already borne fruit in the Harzburg Front of October 1931, a grouping of the various conservative forces on the political right. The Front brought the Nazi party welcome funds and, ironically, gave it a certain respectability, despite the violence of Hitler's brownshirts who were currently trying to terrorize their opponents into submission. The July 1932 election indicated how far the National Socialists had gained in popularity; they doubled their previous vote and won twice as many seats in the Reichstag. There was, however, nothing inevitable about the Nazi advance. How dependent it was on the economic situation was revealed by the returns of November 1932, when an improvement in conditions saw a swing of over four per cent away from the NSDAP and a loss of 34 seats.

Yet only two months later, Hitler was to take office as Chancellor. His success was not, therefore, simply a matter of popular support. It owed as much to his skill as an opportunist in outmanoeuvring a set of conservative politicians who thought they could render him harmless by inviting him into office. Events were to prove that they had totally misjudged Hitler and the situation.

Hitler becomes Chancellor, January 1933

Paul Von Hindenberg, the ageing Weimar President, refused for some time to acknowledge the popularity of Hitler and the Nazis. He tried by juggling his ministerial appointments to keep the conservative character of government, knowing that if the Nazis were admitted to power they would destroy the Weimar Republic. In the four years from 1930 to 1933, three different Chancellors tried to govern through a series of coalitions. Some Nazis grew impatient and urged Hitler to use the SA to overthrow the government by force. Hitler refused. Whatever his ultimate designs, he wanted to come to power by legal means. He had said this as early as 1924. Reflecting on the failure of his illegal putsch, he had declared: 'Instead of working to achieve power by an armed coup, we will have to hold our noses and enter the Reichstag. Sooner or later we will have a majority, and after that – Germany.'

Eventually in January 1933, Hindenberg reluctantly agreed to appoint Hitler as Chancellor but only after he had been assured by Franz von Papen and other cabinet ministers that Hitler would be far less dangerous in office than out, since he would effectively be under the control of the other parties in the government. 'We have him boxed in,' they claimed. But they were hopelessly wrong. Within two months of taking up the Chancellorship, Hitler introduced an Enabling Act which suspended the Weimar constitution and granted him full power to govern in his own right. Two events formed the prelude to this: the burning of the Reichstag building and Nazi success in what was to prove the last Reichstag election.

The Reichstag fire, February 1933

In his 'Appeal to the German People', which he issued on the night he became Chancellor in January, Hitler had declared 'merciless war on spiritual, political and cultural nihilism. Germany must not and will not sink into Communist anarchy.' A month later he was provided with a literally glowing opportunity to put his resolution into practice when a crazed Dutch Communist set fire to the Reichstag building in Berlin. The arsonist, Marinus van der Lubbe, was acting alone, but it was not difficult for the Nazis to denounce it as part of a large-scale Red plot. Watching the fire on the night of 27 February, Hitler became hysterically angry. He screeched: 'This fire is a

God-given signal. It is the work of the Reds. We must crush these murderous pests with an iron fist.'

The Reichstag election, March 1933

Joseph Goebbels, the Nazi Propaganda Minister, and his team immediately picked up the Führer's cue. Skilfully using the atmosphere of fear and uncertainty that the fire had created in the run-up to the Reichstag elections in March, they mounted an aggressive campaign, asserting that only a strong Nazi government led by Hitler could save Germany from a Red revolution. Hermann Goering used the SA to terrorize the other parties into virtual silence. It further helped the Nazis that their leader, Adolf Hitler, was already Chancellor; this put them in a commanding position politically.

The campaign proved highly successful. The Nazi share of the vote increased from 33 per cent to 44 per cent and its number of seats rose from 196 to 288. Now that it was beyond question that the Nazis had far more popular support than any other party, resistance to Hitler within the government collapsed.

Why so many Germans came to support the Nazis

A number of factors came together in the early 1930s to make the Nazis the most appealing of the parties to the German electorate. The Weimar Republic had come increasingly to be judged as a failure. Defectors from the ineffectual moderate parties turned to the extremes of the right or left. The intense nationalism of the Nazi Party proved of greater attraction than the pro-Soviet bias of the German Communists. Many patriotic Germans were attracted to Nazism as the great protector of the nation against the Bolshevik (Communist) menace.

It was also noticeable that new voters, coming mainly from the younger population, were drawn to Hitler's populist image; to many of them he gave the impression of truly understanding the German people and their needs. The unemployed, too, saw hope in the Nazi promises of salvation. A typical unemployed labourer remarked, 'I had lost all I possessed through bad economic conditions. And so, early in 1930, I joined the National Socialist Party.'

The breadth of Hitler's appeal as a leader for all Germans was evident in his winning over the large landowner class whose organization, the *Landbund*, committed itself in 1931 to vote for the Nazis. It was also significant that the dissatisfaction of German industrialists with the mistakes of successive Weimar governments led this highly influential class to drop its earlier objections to the Nazi movement by the early 1930s.

What Germans of all classes admired was Hitler's unyielding stand on the rights of Germany as a nation in Europe. His passionate but reasoned argument for cancelling those clauses of the Versailles Treaty that had humiliated Germany, and his promise to support the appeals of the millions of Germans, who by the terms of the 1919 peace settlement had been placed under foreign governments not of their choosing, struck a chord with all those who had felt let down by the Weimar Republic's inept showing as a defender of German interests abroad.

The Enabling Act, March 1933

In *Mein Kampf*, Hitler had insisted that 'in the smallest as in the greatest problems, one person must have absolute authority and bear all responsibility.' It was, he said, a basic principle of Nazism. Following the election results, he was now free to turn principle into practice. Yet even when making himself absolute, he did it in a legal way. Knowing that, under the Weimar constitution, he needed a two-thirds majority to make major changes in the State, he used a mixture of bribery and threat to dissuade opponents from attending the Reichstag. The result was that the Enabling Act, which would allow him to govern without the Reichstag, was passed by 441 votes to 94. In effect, the Reichstag had voted away its power. There was now no restriction on his personal authority or that of the party he led.

Hitler had no qualms about destroying the power of the Reichstag. It had served its purpose. From now on it would simply be a chamber for endorsing his policies and a platform from which he could address the nation. The truth was he detested democracy, which he condemned as being 'Jewish and un-German'.

Hitler was quick to build on his success. Within a year of the Enabling Act, he had destroyed the trade unions, brought the *Länder*, the parliaments in all the individual German states, under total Nazi control and, by outlawing all opposition groups, turned Germany into a one-party state. The end of democracy was vividly described by the Nazi President of the Württemberg parliament:

> The government will brutally beat down all who oppose it. We do not say an eye for an eye, a tooth for a tooth. No, he who knocks out one of our eyes will get his head chopped off, and he who knocks out one of our teeth will get his jaw bashed in.

The Night of the Long Knives, June 1934

In order to forestall any challenge that might come from within his own party while he was establishing his hold on the nation, Hitler launched a violent purge in the summer of 1934. In what was later dubbed 'the Night of the Long Knives', he moved to rid himself of Ernst Röhm, the leader of the SA, and Hitler's comrade since the days of the Munich putsch. Hitler feared that Röhm, who had put forward a plan for merging the SA with the *Reichswehr* (the German army), was intending a putsch of his own. Röhm's real intentions are unclear, but, rather than wait for him to act, a group of army generals concocted a fake order, appearing to come from him, in which he instructed his SA forces to prepare for a strike against Hitler and the army.

On the night of 30 June 1934, described by Hitler as the 'blackest day' of his life, he personally oversaw the arrest of thousands of SA 'traitors', including Röhm. Some 200 were immediately shot. It was Hitler's hope that Röhm would accept his disgrace and commit suicide. A loaded pistol was placed in his cell. When it became clear that he was not prepared to use it, two guards came in and shot him dead at point-blank range. Hitler issued a public statement: 'The former Chief of Staff, Röhm, was given the opportunity to draw the consequences of his treacherous behaviour. He did not do so and was thereupon shot.' He told the Reichstag members:

> I gave the order to shoot those most guilty of this treason, and I further gave the order to burn out down to the raw flesh the ulcers of our internal well poisoning. If anyone asks why I did not resort to the regular courts of justice for conviction of the offenders, then all I can say is this: in this hour I was responsible for the fate of the German people, and thereby I became the supreme judge of the German people.
>
> (Hitler, July 1934)

It was a justification which Hitler would use, and the German people would accept, throughout the period of the Third Reich. 'The Night of the Long Knives' showed Hitler's utter ruthlessness. It also illustrated the jockeying for position among the power groups in the new Nazi Germany. The army, which had backed Hitler all the way, had asserted their authority over their chief rival, the SA.

Hitler becomes Reich President, August 1934

In August 1934, following the death of Hindenberg, Hitler added the Presidency to his Chancellorship. His supreme power was recognized in his adoption of the title *Führer*, which from then on was the way he was formally addressed. Two weeks later, in a plebiscite asking the people whether they approved Hitler's extension of power, 30 million Germans voted 'yes'.

A vital feature of Hitler's becoming President was that he inherited Hindenberg's position as 'Supreme Commander of the armed forces'. Hitler was now absolute ruler of Germany, politically and militarily. His power was even further entrenched when the German army adopted an oath of 'unconditional loyalty to the person of the *Führer*', to be taken by all those in the armed services. From now on the loyalty of the military was to Hitler personally, not simply to him as head of state. Interestingly, this move was initiated not by Hitler but by the army leaders. What they wanted was to create a special relationship with Hitler that would establish the independence of the army from the Nazi Party. The army minister, General Werner von Blomberg, who had pushed for this, remarked: 'We swore the oath on the flag to Hitler as *Führer* of the German people, not as head of the National Socialist Party.' From now until 1945, Hitler and the German armed forces had a special relationship. This was ultimately to prove tragic, since the army's loyalty to the *Führer* personally prevented their challenging his decisions even when these were militarily absurd.

In 1936, Hitler was able to boast:

> After three years, great are the successes which providence has let me attain for our Fatherland in these three years. In all areas of our national, political and

economic life, our position has been improved ... In these three years Germany has regained its honour, found belief again, overcome its greatest economic distress and has finally ushered in a new cultural assent.

(Hitler, March 1936)

How far the people agreed was shown in the elections of March 1936. Hitler won 98.9 per cent of the vote. It has to be noted that this was in an election in which only the Nazis were allowed to stand, but even allowing for this mockery of democracy, the fact was that the overwhelming mass of the German people applauded what Hitler had done for the nation since 1933. One of his great successes, they believed, was to have made Germany a proud nation again by his courageous and skilful foreign policy, a theme dealt with in the next chapter.

03 the Third Reich expands

This chapter will cover:

- Hitler's ambitions abroad
- how Germany expanded, 1933–9
- the reaction of the European powers to Germany
- the international crises of the 1930s
- why war came in 1939.

Hitler's foreign policy

Much of Hitler's popularity down to 1933 derived from his fierce condemnation of the Versailles Treaty, which in the eyes of nationalists had humiliated Germany. This was an exaggeration. As peace treaties go, Versailles had not been particularly severe on Germany, but it was good politics for the Nazis to suggest that it had. When, therefore, Hitler, came to power in 1933 it seemed that he was now in a position to tear up the treaty. But at first he showed caution. He was realistic enough to appreciate that Germany needed economic and military recovery before it could contemplate an aggressive foreign policy. Moreover, the terms of the Treaty were still in force and he did not yet know how strongly France and Britain would defend the 1919 settlement.

Germany proposed that the terms of the Versailles Treaty should be modified so that the new Nazi state could rebuild its armed services to the same level as the other European nations. The British and Italians were willing to discuss the question, but the French objected. This enabled Hitler to act as the injured party. In October 1933, he ordered the withdrawal of Germany from both the League of Nations and the disarmament talks at Geneva, claiming that if his country could not be treated as an equal it made no sense for it to remain in these organizations.

The other powers did nothing in response. Poland, worried now that the uncertainties among the Western European powers would leave her vulnerable, began talks with Berlin. These resulted in a ten-year non-aggression pact being signed between Germany and Poland in January 1934. It was also in 1934 that Germany and Italy drew closer together as symbolized by Hitler's visit to Venice as the personal guest of Mussolini.

Germany begins to rearm, 1935

Buoyed up by such developments, Hitler took his boldest step yet by rearming Germany in defiance of the restrictions imposed under the Versailles Treaty. In 1935, he introduced conscription with a view to increasing the German army to half a million men, five times the figure allowed under the Treaty.

This time there was some response among the powers, but of a very limited kind. They formed the Stresa Front. This was an agreement signed between Britain, France and Italy. But the

Stresa Front did no more than restate its commitment to peace through negotiation and issue a mild reprimand to Germany for rearming in disregard of Versailles. What made the Front so ineffectual was that one of its members, Italy, was currently engaged in an aggressive takeover of Abyssinia. Rather than oppose what was plainly an illegal act, France and Britain negotiated the Hoare-Laval Pact, an agreement with Mussolini's fascist state that left it in control of the greater part of Abyssinia.

The failure of France and Britain to act more forcefully towards Germany and Italy was a result not so much of moral cowardice as of military weakness. The plain truth was that in 1935 neither country was ready for serious military action. In Britain's case, its forces had shrunk not grown. Troop numbers had fallen from 3.5 million in 1919 to below 200,000 in 1930. Defence spending, which had stood at £700 million in 1920, had dropped to £115 million in 1935.

German remilitarization of the Rhineland, 1936

Hitler did not know such details but it was becoming evident that, for whatever reasons, his western neighbours were not ready for a fight. This encouraged his expansionist ideas. His next move came in 1936 when he moved troops into the Rhineland, an area that according to the Versailles Treaty had to remain demilitarized in order to safeguard France's eastern frontier. This was Hitler's most provocative act yet, and he fully expected the French and British to resist. Indeed, he had given instructions to his troops to withdraw should this happen. But, apart from making formal diplomatic protests, France and Britain again did nothing. Addressing the troops before they set off for the Rhineland, Hitler remarked: 'We have no territorial claims to make in Europe.' He was not being ironic. All his actions so far had been the reclaiming of German sovereignty. Nowhere had Germany invaded across national borders.

The forming of the Axis, 1936

1936 was also the year that Hitler looked for formal allies. In *Mein Kampf*, he had spoken of France and Britain as natural allies of Germany. But recent events had for the moment ruled out the likelihood of an alliance with them. Hitler had been

figure 3 map showing German expansion 1933–9

outraged to learn that the British Ambassador in Berlin had sent a report to London describing the Third Reich as being 'in the hands of adventurers'. He had retorted that the British Empire had been built by adventurers but was now 'governed merely by incompetents'. Given such strains, the obvious German choice for an ally in Europe, was Mussolini's Italy. As dictators, *Il Duce* (Italian for 'the leader') and the *Führer*, clearly had much in common. The example of Mussolini's fascist seizure of power in Italy was often quoted by Hitler and the Nazis as an inspiration.

In October 1936, talks with Count Ciano, Mussolini's son in-law and Foreign Minister, during which Hitler described Mussolini as 'the leading statesman in the world' prepared the way for a formal association. The press of both countries ran campaigns stressing the bonds that linked Italy and Germany: a common political philosophy, a deep national pride, a shared hatred of Bolshevism, and each nation led by a man of destiny and genius.

The term chosen to describe the great bond that now united Germany and Italy was coined by Mussolini. He spoke of the two countries forming an 'Axis'. It was meant to portray strength and solidarity; Mussolini also referred to it as 'the pact of steel'. The Axis was soon expanded to include the major Asian power, Japan, whose imperial, militaristic government had many of the features of western fascism. The three-power agreement took the form of the anti-Comintern Pact. Germany, Italy and Japan declared their common opposition to the Comintern, the agency of the USSR for promoting international revolution.

The Spanish Civil War, 1936–9

Axis co-operation was soon evident in the Spanish Civil War. In 1936, General Franco led his Nationalist forces, representing Catholic, conservative Spain, in rebellion against the Republican government, which had the support of a combination of anarchists, regional separatists and Communists. A bitter three-year conflict followed.

Italian and German units aided Franco's armies, while the USSR gave support to the Republicans. For Hitler, the attraction of the war was that it offered a training ground for German forces, particularly the *Luftwaffe*, which tried out its bombing techniques on civilian targets. The most infamous example was the destruction of the Basque town of Guernica, which was attacked by German and Italian squadrons. The atrocity was immortalized in an angry abstract painting by the celebrated Spanish artist, Pablo Picasso.

The *Anschluss*, 1938

It was not surprising that Hitler should have dreamed of incorporating Austria, the land of his birth, into the Third Reich. It was really a question of when and how it would happen. That such a move was forbidden by the Versailles settlement was now merely a technical difficulty. After all, German rearmament and the militarization of the Rhineland had been similarly forbidden and that had not stopped Hitler going ahead with them. The impetus for the *Anschluss* (the German term for the incorporation of Austria into greater Germany) came from the Austrian Nazis. Since Hitler's coming to power in 1933, they had been planning to take control in their own country. As had happened in Germany, they used strong-arm tactics to press their cause and to silence opposition. Their claim was that they wanted to exercise their right of self-determination by making Austria part of the Third Reich.

This perfectly suited Hitler's case. He demanded that Kurt von Schuschnigg, the Austrian Chancellor, accept Nazis into his government. In an attempt to save his country from violation, Schuschnigg went to see Hitler at Berchtesgaden, the *Führer's* residence in southern Bavaria. He walked into a storm. Although a guest, he was subjected to constant haranguing and bullying. Hitler told him that in order to win justice for the Austrian Nazis he was quite prepared to start a civil war. On his return to Austria, Schuschnigg continued to resist Hitler's demands, but when German forces massed on the border he resigned to make way for the rabid Nazi, Arthur Seyss-Inquart, as Chancellor. This was the prelude to Hitler's triumphant entry into Austria, which was now declared to be part of Greater Germany. The huge welcome he received, and a referendum held soon after that returned an overwhelming majority in favour of *Anschluss*, appeared to vindicate Hitler's actions. Certainly France and Britain, though concerned by it, were unwilling to intervene.

Hitler raised the *Anschluss* to the level of a great mystical event in which he had participated as an instrument of destiny.

> What has happened in these past weeks is the result of a triumph of an idea, a triumph of will ... above all it is the result of a miracle of faith, for only faith could have moved these mountains ... I believe that it was also God's will that from here [Austria] a boy was to be sent into the Reich, allowed to mature, and elevated to become the nation's *Führer*, thus enabling him to reinvigorate his homeland into the Reich. There is a divine will, and we are its instruments.
>
> (Hitler, April 1938)

It was also to the principle of self-determination that Hitler appealed in the next major European crisis, the Sudetenland issue, a crisis of Hitler's deliberate making.

Germany recovers the Sudetenland, 1938

Czechoslovakia, one of the new states created under the Versailles Treaty, was made up of a variety of ethnic groups. As the nation's title indicated, the preponderant peoples were the Czechs and Slovaks. But together they made up only half the total population; there were significant minorities who were unhappy at being incorporated into a state to which they did not wish to belong. The most vociferous of these were the 3.25 million ethnic Germans of the *Sudetenland* ('southland' in German) who demanded to be reincorporated into Germany. Unsurprisingly, the leaders of the Sudeten Germans, such as Kurt Henlein, were all Nazis.

Hitler eagerly exploited the demand of the Sudeten Germans, for 'self-determination'. He subjected the Czech President, Eduard Benes, and his government to a set of increasingly impossible demands. When Benes went to Germany to argue his country's case, he was treated the same way Schuschnigg had been. Hitler forced him to listen to a shrieking tirade of abuse.

Czechoslovakia had formal protective agreements with the USSR and France, but neither of those countries proved willing to honour its commitment, France because it judged its armies were not yet ready for a European war, the USSR because any Soviet troop movements would have to go through Poland whose government would refuse permission since its own eyes were on Czech territory. That left only Italy and Britain as possible Czech allies. But what was distinctive about both these countries at this time was their determination to avoid being drawn into a European war.

figure 4 map of the regions of Czechoslovakia in 1938

Neville Chamberlain, the British Prime Minister, declared that it was 'fantastic' and 'incredible' that Britain should even contemplate going to war for a far-off country about which his people knew nothing. All Chamberlain's diplomatic efforts, therefore, were devoted to reaching a settlement that would avoid Britain's having to fight. The rights and wrongs of the Czech question did not really come into it.

This attitude played straight into Hitler's hands. When, after a series of diplomatic manoeuvres, the major powers gathered at Munich to resolve the issue, it was already decided. Since no country was prepared to resist Germany militarily, Hitler would get his way. And so it proved. Hitler, Chamberlain, Mussolini and Daladier of France, agreed on a formula, drawn up by Goering, that recognized all Hitler's major demands. Czechoslovakia would have to accept the loss of the Sudetenland or fight on alone. Being in no position to do this, Benes accepted the inevitable, remarking in despair that to protect their own interests the powers had destroyed his country. Within days of the Munich agreement, German troops had entered the Sudetenland to frenetic applause from the local people. The region was now part of Greater Germany.

Interestingly, there was a divergence of attitude among the Nazi leaders over Munich. For Goering it was something of a personal triumph since he had first drafted the plan, for a settlement. Goebbels excitedly declared that 'Germany's prestige has grown enormously. Now we really are a world power again.' Ribbentrop was less enthusiastic. He was put out by the diplomatic success of Goering with whom he had a long-running rivalry. Moreover, he had wanted a war, not a settlement, which would have given the Germans as much of Czechoslovakia as they wanted and would have embarrassed the British, whom he disliked. Ribbentrop was also jealous that Chamberlain had been hailed as the saviour of European peace as he drove through Munich.

Hitler, too, had originally been in favour of a limited war against the Czechs. Gaining the Sudetenland by negotiation rather than by a striking military victory took the edge off his sense of satisfaction. As for the famous piece of paper that he jointly signed at Chamberlain's request, pledging that Britain and Germany would never go to war with each other again, it meant nothing to him. He later said that he agreed to it because the British Prime Minister was obviously a nice old man and he did not want to upset him.

One thing that Hitler felt he had learnt at Munich was how easy it was to push France and Britain around. That was why he was unimpressed by the guarantees those two countries later gave to Poland. On the eve of the outbreak of war in August 1939, he told his generals, 'Our enemies are worms, I saw them at Munich.'

The Polish crisis, 1939

How little Hitler really cared about the whole diplomatic farce he had been through at Munich was clear within months. In March 1939, he simply ignored the settlement and ordered the German occupation of Bohemia and Moravia, a seizure that effectively destroyed the Czechoslovak state. Not having been effectively opposed at any stage in its challenges to Versailles so far, German expansion seemed to have developed a dangerous momentum. European peace and stability were now obviously under threat.

Yet it was arguable that up to March 1939, Germany, while aggressive in attitude, had kept within bounds. None of her claims had been illegal and she had not forced herself on unwilling peoples. Rhinelanders, Austrians and Sudetens had cheered the German armies as they marched in. It is true that Hitler had torn up the Versailles Treaty, but there were many in Europe who believed that the Treaty had been unfair in the first place and that consequently the Germans had every right to reject its provisions. For example, Winston Churchill, as ardent an opponent of Nazism as one could find, acknowledged that the re-occupation of the Rhineland, the incorporation of Austria into the Third Reich, and the reclamation of the Sudetenland were all in keeping with the principle of self-determination which the Allies had made the basis of the peace talks in 1919. Justice and logic suggested that this principle could not be applied to other peoples but then denied to the Germans.

Such thinking became largely irrelevant once Germany went beyond what was acceptable internationally. This came with the German threat to Poland, beginning in the spring of 1939. In the light of Hitler's consistent belief that it was Germany's destiny to take the lands to the east, it was to be expected that Poland would at some point suffer German invasion. That point was fast approaching. The difference between the Polish case and all the others so far was that there were far more Poles living under German control than there were Germans under Polish authority. Hence Germany's demands on Poland were based on force not justice. The principle of self-determination did not apply.

Nevertheless, the pressurizing of Poland followed the, by now, familiar pattern. Germany demanded that Poland give up all authority over German peoples living in Polish occupied areas. Hitler made much of Danzig, which, though officially designated a free city, was, he claimed, under Poland's control. When Polish ministers attempted to discuss matters with German officials they were insulted and bawled at. Hitler was bent on taking Poland. Short of total surrender to German demands, there was nothing the Poles could do to put off the invasion that seemed bound to come.

This time there was little of the diplomatic urgency in Europe that had produced the Munich agreement a year earlier. There was a sense of inevitability about things. At least Britain's position was clear. In March 1939, in response to the German seizure of Moravia and Bohemia, which was a direct breach of the Munich agreement, Britain had given formal guarantees that it would come to Poland's aid in the event of a German attack. The irony was that the guarantees were essentially a gesture since Britain did not have the means to defend Poland in 1939. Britain was in no better position to protect the Poles than it had been the Czechs.

That was also how Hitler appeared to think. He had good reason to believe that France and Britain would not oppose him. At each step in the expansion of Germany they had given way. Their policy of 'appeasement' allowed Germany to make very considerable gains with no threat of Anglo-French retaliation. As Hitler saw it, there was no greater reason for Britain going to war over Poland than there had been over Czechoslovakia. If the Allies had been willing to compromise over the Sudeten question, they would surely eventually do the same over Poland.

Hitler's position was a rational one. Neville Chamberlain had frequently expressed a deep horror of war, an attitude shared by the British people who applauded his statesmanship at Munich in pulling Europe back from the brink of war. Why, Hitler was entitled to ask, was fear of war not as powerful in Britain in September 1939 as it had been 12 months earlier at the time of Munich? Part of the answer was that in 1939 Britain and France were resigned to war as well as being marginally better prepared militarily. There was also a sense in which the Allies had reached the end of their tether. It was an accumulative thing. Whatever the merits of the Polish question, it seemed to represent a stage too far in German expansion.

Another factor was that, shortly before Britain and France declared war on Germany in September 1939, there had been an extraordinary twist in the diplomatic shape of Europe. In August 1939 the two great ideological enemies, Nazi Germany and the Soviet Union, who on Stalin's own admission had for years been 'pouring buckets of filth over each other' in a bitter propaganda war, had entered into a non-aggression pact. It was a diplomatic development that staggered the rest of the world. Europe's two deadliest foes, bitterly divided by race and ideology and each sworn to the other's destruction, had become allies. As one British diplomat remarked, 'Europe's isms [i.e., fasc*ism* and Commun*ism*] have become wasms.'

This amazing turnabout in Nazi-Soviet relations, which left Germany free to occupy all of Europe up to the Soviet border,

RENDEZVOUS

The Nazi-Soviet Pact as interpreted by David Low of the *Evening Standard* in his cartoon of 20 September 1939.

Hitler is saying, 'The scum of the earth, I believe.' Stalin is saying, 'The bloody assassin of the workers, I presume.'

Courtesy: Solo Syndication

convinced the French and British that what they had always struggled to prevent, the domination of Europe by one nation, was now a reality. Their only recourse was to go to war against that nation.

The Nazi-Soviet Pact, August 1939

From the time of the Nazis' coming to power in Germany in 1933, Stalin had tried to persuade Britain and France into forming a defensive alliance with the USSR against the Third Reich. But his overtures had been largely ignored. He interpreted this rejection as part of a Western plan to gang up against the Soviet Union. This led him to view the Munich agreement as a cover under which the capitalist powers of Western Europe had plotted to attack the Soviet Union. On the principle of 'if you can't beat 'em, join 'em', Stalin switched his attentions to Germany, accepting from Hitler a proposal that talks should be held with a view to creating some form of alliance. It offered the prospect of providing the USSR with the security it desired. The main attraction for Hitler at this stage was that an alliance with the USSR would make it easier to defeat Poland. It would also secure Germany's eastern borders, and thus free her to take on France and Britain should they declare war.

The result was that on 23 August 1939, Ribbentrop and Molotov, the respective German and Soviet foreign secretaries, met in Moscow to sign the Nazi-Soviet Pact. When Hitler received news that the signing had taken place successfully, he slapped his knee in a characteristic gesture of delight. The agreement pledged Germany and the USSR to remain at peace with each other for ten years. In secret proposals, they also agreed to carve up Poland between them. This the two countries promptly proceeded to do. In the event, the ten-year peace did not even reach two years since in June 1941 Hitler was to unleash 'Operation Barbarossa' against the USSR. However, at the time it suited both Hitler and Stalin to project the Pact as a major diplomatic coup. Hitler thought that it would lead Poland to give up without a fight and help deter the Western powers from declaring war; they would see how foolhardy it was to challenge an even stronger Germany.

But foolhardy or not, that was how Britain and France chose to react. Immediately following the news that German armies had crossed into Poland on 1 September, the two Western allies delivered an ultimatum demanding their withdrawal. When Germany declined to respond, France and Britain declared war on 3 September. Hitler's bluff had been called. The future of the Third Reich and of Europe was now to be determined by armed conflict.

Hitler's responsibility for the war

It used to be generally thought that Hitler had a master plan by which he plotted to reverse the results of the Great War and assert German control over the whole of Europe as a step to world domination. Few historians any longer see things as simply as that. The prevailing view now is that Hitler in foreign affairs, as in domestic ones, was an opportunist who responded to events rather than directing them. It is true that he had broad objectives. For example, he wanted Germany to recover its military strength, he longed to destroy Bolshevism, and he dreamed of *Lebensraum* (literally 'living space', which meant the taking over and settlement of Eastern Europe by Germans). But these were aims, not detailed plans. His style was to play upon the weaknesses of others and see how far he could push them. He preferred to get his way by threats and resorted to war only when his threats were not enough.

When we trace the expansion of Germany under Hitler, it appears to have a neat shape to it, culminating in war in 1939. But this is a pattern we place upon it afterwards because we know what is going to happen. At the time the events occurred, there was no certainty that they would turn out the way they did. Had those involved responded differently to his demands from the way they actually did, Hitler would no doubt have dropped or changed his demands. This was particularly true of the mid-1930s when he expected Britain and France to be far firmer in resisting his moves than they were. Their appeasement of Germany made him bolder and more ambitious.

The only long-term plan of Hitler's that can be clearly detected is his desire to seize the lands of Slav Europe and exploit them to serve Germany's needs. There is no evidence that he had hostile designs on Western Europe. He admired the British Empire and believed that French civilization had much to offer. Provided they got rid of their Jews, both countries could have a worthwhile future. France and Britain had, of course, helped to impose the Versailles Treaty, but if they now allowed him to cancel out those clauses which were unfair to Germany, Hitler was prepared to live and let live. Apart from Alsace-Lorraine, he had no claims on French territory and none on British. Whether appetite would have grown by what it fed on, giving him designs on the French and British empires, remains a matter of speculation. Such aims were certainly not part of his thinking in the 1930s.

The Hossbach Memorandum, 1937

A piece of evidence that has aroused considerable debate is the Hossbach Memorandum dating from November 1937. It was in that month that Hitler held a special meeting attended by Blomberg, the Minister for War, Neurath, the Foreign Minister, and the three service chiefs: Fritsch of the army, Raeder of the navy, and Goering of the *Luftwaffe*. Notes of the discussion were jotted down by Colonel Hossbach, Hitler's adjutant. The meeting, which had been called to discuss supply problems, appears to have became a two-hour rambling monologue by the *Führer* in which he suggested that, in view of the current tensions over foreign policy in France, Britain and Italy, there might well be a war in Europe in the near future and that Germany ought, therefore, to be prepared to make pre-emptive strikes to safeguard her position.

Some historians later seized on these notes, known as the Hossbach Memorandum, as proof that Hitler was planning a war in Western Europe. Indeed the Memorandum was introduced at the Nuremberg war-crimes hearings (1945–6) as evidence of Germany's warlike intentions. However, nowhere in the notes were specific plans mentioned by Hitler, nor did he ask his hearers to draw up any. It may well be that, as one eminent historian suggested, Hitler was simply 'daydreaming', something he constantly did in his table talk. Rather than to plan a war, what is much more likely is that Hitler called the meeting for domestic reasons. He was worried that the enthusiasm for spending on rearmament was declining among Germany's economic planners. The Hossbach meeting, therefore, was a wake-up call to impress his listeners with the need to press on with rearmament. It is significant that when Hossbach later showed the notes to Hitler he expressed no interest and declined to read them.

Hitler, then, did not originally want war with France and Britain – nor did he plan it. It served no German interest. He had no wish to attack westwards. What he wanted was the east, the lands inhabited by the sub-human Slavs. His racial theories justified the notion that the people of the east could be used as slave labour to build the greater German Reich at the lowest cost.

If one steps outside the passion which usually accompanies the discussion, one can see that there was often logic and justice in some of the Nazi claims between 1933 and 1939. As was acknowledged by people like Churchill, Germany had been unfairly treated at Versailles. It was not so much that the terms were harsh; indeed compared with some settlements, they might be thought lenient. Germany lost its colonies, it is true, but its integrity as a sovereign state was untouched. What angered Germans was that they had been denied one of the universal principles for which the Allies claimed to have fought the war – the right of self-determination. It could be argued, therefore, that, with the exception of the attack on Poland, which was clearly an act of unprovoked aggression, German expansion between 1933 and 1939 was a series of wrongs being righted in accordance with a universally accepted principle.

Another key consideration is that until the post-Munich period, moderate political opinion in Europe was markedly sympathetic towards Germany. That was where Communism came in. Since 1917, Bolshevik Russia had called for the violent overthrow of the capitalist nations of Europe. We now know that there had been no possibility of this. The Soviet Union did not have the strength, even if it had had the will. But at the time the threat seemed real enough and it was taken seriously in Western Europe. That was why many in France and Britain welcomed the growth of a strong, anti-Communist Germany. They saw it as a barrier to the spread of Bolshevism westward. The Soviet menace made many in Western Europe conciliatory towards Nazi Germany.

In the end, what a person does is more important than why he does it. The only consistent theme identifiable in Hitler's turgid ramblings is that Germany had a providential mission to take Eastern Europe. Nowhere is there a hint of a desire to take on the French and British. Insofar as any war can be an accident, the struggle that broke out in Western Europe in September 1939 was one.

04 Nazi Germany at war, 1939–42

This chapter will cover:

- the attitude of Germans towards the war
- the key episodes in the war in Europe up to the end of 1941
- why Hitler was more concerned to defeat Russia than Britain
- the problems Germany had with Italy
- the reasons for Germany going to war with the USA.

Germany at the outbreak of war in 1939

The announcement of war in Germany in 1914 had been received rapturously. The mood was much more sombre in 1939. There was no open show of opposition, but foreign observers remarked on how reflective, even strained, many ordinary Germans were. The crowds on the streets were thinner than usual when Hitler drove to the Reichstag to announce the war, and the cheering of the deputies in the chamber seemed more muted than normal despite Goebbels having packed the place with party members to fill up the spaces left by those deputies who had already been called up for military service.

Without saying so publicly, a good number of the population may have felt that Germany had gone too far this time in upsetting the Western European powers and putting herself at risk. Memories of the horrors of the 1914–18 war on both the fighting and home fronts were still fresh in the minds of many. They did not want a repeat. An American commentator wondered how Hitler could contemplate going to war with his people 'so dead against it'. A minority were so unsure of Germany's position that they even contemplated removing Hitler, by assassination if need be. Significant members of the military shared the unease.

The uncertainties among the Germans were expressed in a report from Upper Franconia: 'Trust in the *Führer* will now probably be subjected to its hardest acid test.' This described the position perfectly. Hitler would be judged on how well the war went. He had, after all, in the eyes of the German people been their saviour so far. As the majority saw it, he had ended unemployment, stabilized the economy, inspired the young, raised the nation's prestige, and given the people back their sense of self-worth. An unsuccessful war could shatter these achievements, but a successful one could make him an even greater hero. Everything depended on the outcome of the military struggle in which the nation was now engaged.

The key moments and main phases of the war, 1939–41

1939	German seizure of Poland Britain and France declare war on Germany
1939–40	The 'phony war'
1940	German invasion of Denmark and Norway
	German seizure of Holland and Belgium Dunkirk evacuation Fall of France Italy enters war as ally of Germany
1940–1	German aerial attack on Britain
1940–2	North Africa campaigns
1941	German invasion of Russia USA declares war on Japan Germany declares war on USA

The defeat of Poland, September 1939

Although Britain and France had taken the initiative by declaring war on Germany, their lack of military strength denied them the means of making any significant move. What was certain was that they could not directly help Poland, on whose behalf they had gone to war. They judged that the best they could do was wait to be attacked themselves and then counter-attack where possible. Cursing themselves for their failure to re-arm in the 1930s, the British and French pre-occupied themselves with preparing for the German aerial bombardment they were sure would come.

In a sense, Germany's attack on Poland was a joint venture with the USSR. Under the terms of the Nazi-Soviet Pact, the two countries had agreed to divide Poland between them, Russia to take the east, Germany the west. Both countries duly prepared to seize their respective areas. Germany's attack was directed by General Halder. Only a year earlier, this same general had been so unsure of Hitler's policy in seizing Czechoslovakia that he had seriously considered leading a coup against the *Führer*. But now all Halder's doubts had gone. Expressing absolute faith in Hitler's decisions, Halder told his officers that Poland was to be 'smashed in record time'.

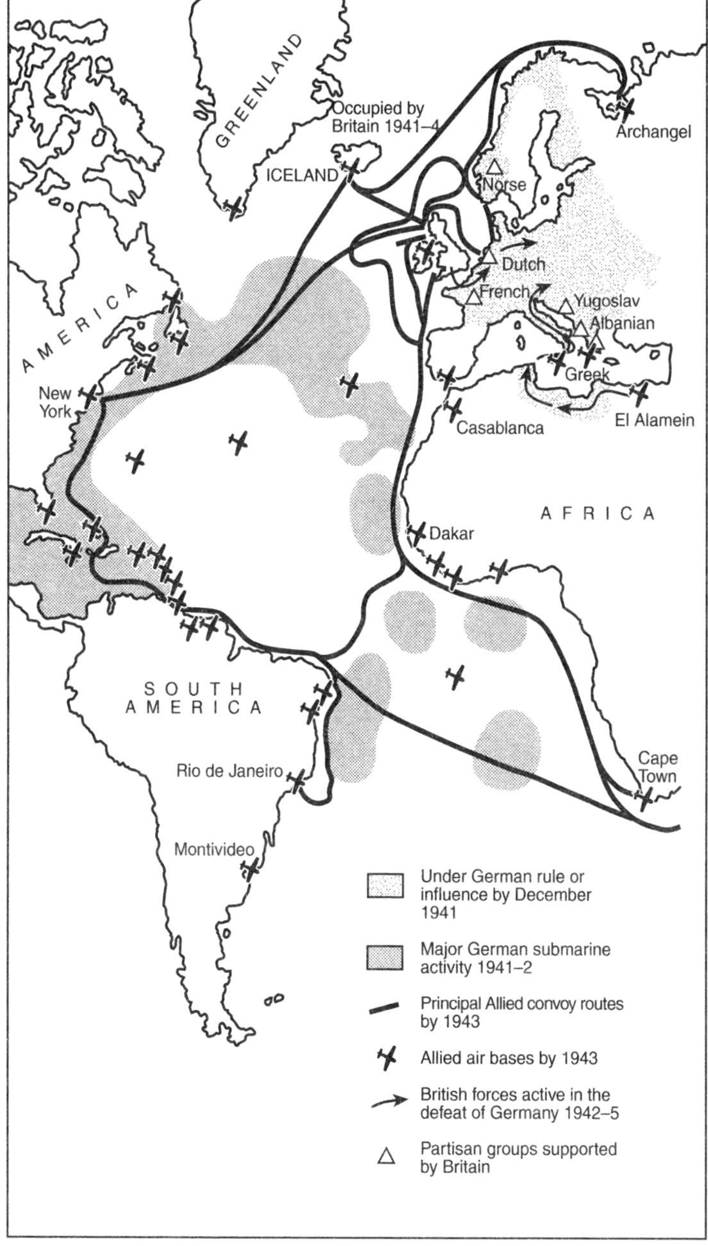

figure 5 map showing the main developments in the Second World War

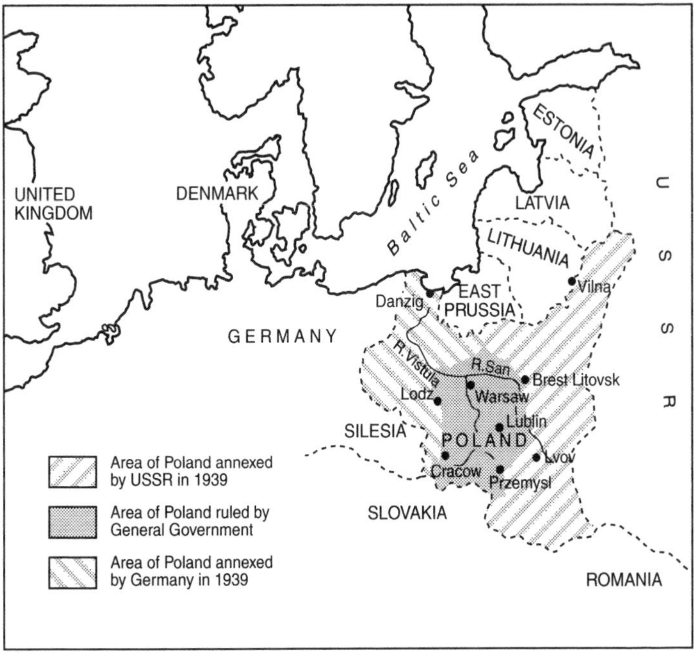

figure 6 map showing partition of Poland between Germany and the Soviet Union

The army fulfilled the command. Poland fell within weeks. With no foreign help to call on, the Poles were simply no match for the German forces. Subjected to a series of *Blitzkrieg* attacks, involving rapid panzer (German tank) assaults, backed by dive-bombing stuker aircraft, Polish resistance proved gallant but hopeless. Nazi Germany and Soviet Russia then proceeded to divide Poland between them.

The 'phony war', 1939–40

With Poland defeated, Hitler could relax and contemplate the war in the west against France and Britain. Hitler had intended attacking France by the end of the year, but was told by his senior generals they would not be ready until the following spring. So for some months there was an interlude, later referred to by the Americans as the 'phony war'. It was in this period that Hitler put out peace feelers. Between October 1939 and June 1940, the British government received offers of an end to the war if it accepted German terms. Some Cabinet members were tempted but nothing came of it.

The invasion of Norway, 1940

The phony war came to an abrupt end in April 1940 with Germany's invasion of Norway. The decision to invade was an economic one. Hitler was finally persuaded by Admiral Raeder, head of the German navy, that to avoid the valuable mineral and ore deposits in Scandinavia falling into British hands, German forces should occupy Norway, taking Denmark as a stepping stone on the way. The British responded by sending a task force to Norway but it was too small to prevent the Germans overrunning the country. The British failure led directly to the replacement of Neville Chamberlain by Winston Churchill, the inveterate anti-Nazi, as Prime Minister.

The fall of France, May–June 1940

In May 1940, having being delayed for a time by the need to send troops to Greece and Yugoslavia (two Balkan countries that had come into the war on the Allied side), Hitler was ready to take Western Europe. In a series of rapid and brilliantly planned moves, German forces swept through Holland, Belgium, Luxembourg and into northern France. The speed of it was breathtaking, so much so that with the remnants of the French army and the British Expeditionary Force (BEF) compressed into a narrow area backing onto the Channel port of Dunkirk, Hitler ordered his panzer units to delay their pursuit when they were only 24 km (15 miles) from Dunkirk.

His aim was to consolidate the German position, but it proved a fateful decision. The two-day delay enabled the BEF, despite being continually strafed from the air, to make a desperate but ultimately successful evacuation of 330,000 troops from Dunkirk, along with a large number of French soldiers. Churchill, the new British PM, was quick to point out that, while retreats are not victories, the saving of the BEF had created the biggest lift in national morale since the beginning of the war. It strengthened Britain's resolve to fight on. Hitler had made a major error. The troops lifted from the beaches would return to fight in Italy, the western desert, and in the reconquest of Western Europe.

But Germany did not realize this at the time. By June, seven weeks after the Western offensive had been launched, Paris had fallen and the French had surrendered. Hitler made a brief visit to Paris to enjoy his triumph. He admired much of the capital's architecture but vowed to turn Berlin into an even grander city. In a symbolic act of retribution, he ordered that the formal French surrender should take place in the same railway carriage in which the German generals had signed the armistice in 1918. The elation felt by the German people at the great victory in the West was intense. When Hitler returned in triumph to Berlin from Paris, he was met with boundless adulation. To universal acclaim, General Keitel described him as 'the greatest warlord in history'. A member of the vast crowd who roared their approval captured the mood: 'If an increase in feeling for Adolf Hitler is still possible, it has become reality with the day of his return to Berlin. In the face of such greatness all pettiness and grumbling are silenced.'

That Britain was still holding out seemed of little consequence in the face of such triumph. In any case, Hitler's thoughts were not primarily about Britain. His eyes looked eastwards. So striking had been the success of his forces in taking Western Europe that it sharpened his desire to embark on his ultimate objective, the taking of the Slav East. But, until Germany was ready for that, it made sense to continue with plans for the defeat of Britain.

The aerial attack on Britain, August 1940–May 1941

In preparation for an invasion of Britain, Goering ordered the *Luftwaffe* to gain control of the skies over the Channel and southern Britain. But in the six days, 13–18 August, 236 German planes were shot down while British losses were only 95. This led the *Luftwaffe* to redirect its attacks onto London rather than the RAF bases. This was another crucial German error since it allowed the airfield crews to repair the damaged planes. Despite being stretched to the limit, the British pilots won the battle of the skies. Between 30 August and 7 September, the RAF lost 185 planes to the *Luftwaffe*'s 225. On 15 September, in the last major engagement of what became known as the Battle of Britain, the aircraft losses were German 56, British 26. Early in October, Hitler suspended the invasion plan indefinitely.

He turned instead to a new strategy; British resistance was to be undermined by terror. The *Luftwaffe* began to attack civilian targets. London and other selected cities were subjected to a sustained series of nightly bombing raids. These were at their heaviest between September 1940 and May 1941. For over a hundred nights during that period, London suffered intensive attacks in what became known as the Blitz. But, although the normal pattern of life and work was disrupted, civilian morale held. Intermittent German raids continued after May 1941, but their numbers noticeably fell as the *Luftwaffe* turned its attention to planning Germany's attack on the USSR.

The invasion of the USSR, 1941

In retrospect, the timing of Operation Barbarossa, the code-name for the attack on the Soviet Union, seems ill-judged. Why did Hitler not wait until after Britain had fallen? However, at the time, the German belief was that a successful attack on the USSR would hasten Britain's collapse since the hopelessness of her position in Europe would be revealed. Totally without allies, Britain would accept there was no point in continuing to resist the inevitable.

Hitler's attitude was, of course, based on deeper considerations. In his eyes, victory over the Soviet Union would destroy 'Jewish-Bolshevism' and confirm Nazi Germany's destiny as a great imperial power. His dream of taking the East and so provide the German people with their rightful *Lebensraum* ('living space') would be fulfilled. 'What India was for England,' he claimed, 'the Eastern territory will be for us.' And so, tearing up the Nazi-Soviet Pact, Hitler unleashed a massive attack on Russia on 22 June 1941.

Hitler declared that the world would hold its breath when it witnessed Barbarossa. He had every right to be dramatic. It was a huge enterprise, unprecedented in the history of warfare. Over 3 million troops, half a million motorized vehicles, 4,000 tanks, 3,000 aircraft, and 600,000 horses were drawn up.

Yet it was not this great array that gave the invaders the initial advantage. Indeed, in terms of simple logistics, the Soviet Union had the larger forces. It matched Germany in the number of troops, had four times the number of tanks, and three times the number of aircraft. What made the Soviet Union incapable of effective defence in the early days of the war was Stalin's mental paralysis.

Despite the overwhelming evidence of a massive build-up on the Soviet Union's western borders, Stalin refused to believe in the attack even after it had started. For days he locked himself away, incapable of giving rational commands. When at last he did pull himself together he began to show the strength of leadership for which he became renowned later in the war. But his inertia had given the initiative to Germany. It would take desperate Soviet resistance to win it back.

Two factors explain the German failure to defeat the USSR by the winter of 1941–2. One was the lateness of the launching of Barbarossa. The original plan had been to attack in May 1941. General Halder had said in the previous year: 'If we start in May 1941, we would have five months to finish the job.' However, in the event, the operation had to be delayed in order to allow German forces to be sent to suppress anti-Nazi risings in Yugoslavia and Greece. Although the campaigns were successful, they resulted in the attack on Russia being moved back by some six weeks.

This meant that, in spite of the rapid and crushing advance of German forces, the expected Russian capitulation had not come by the autumn of 1941. Neither Moscow nor Leningrad, though heavily besieged by then, had fallen. It was now that fate intervened on Russia's side. The thick mud of a torrential autumn was followed by the snow and ice of one of the severest winters in Russian memory. German movement slowed to a dead halt. Russian forces were able to regroup and begin a counter attack under Marshal Zhukov in December 1941. Germany was now involved in a struggle on the Eastern Front that would decide the outcome of the war itself.

War in the Balkans and North Africa, 1940–2

Mussolini, eager to gain Hitler's favour and show that Italy was a powerful military nation, came into the war on Germany's side in June 1940, following the fall of France. There was calculation in this. In 1939, much to Hitler's annoyance, Mussolini had told him that Italy was not ready for war and so would not be joining Germany in the coming struggle in Western Europe. However, now that Germany had carried all before it, Italy was willing to join the war as an ally in the hope of easy pickings. The great irony of all this was that events were

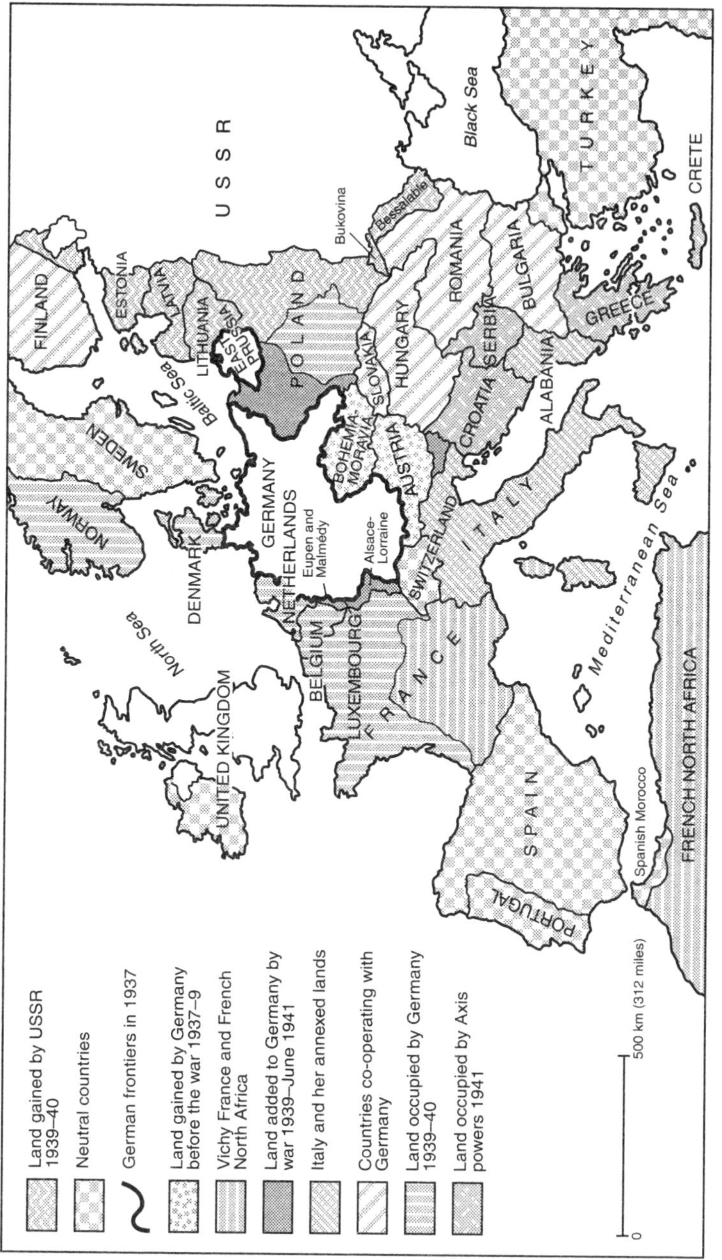

figure 7 map showing the extent of Germany's control over Europe in 1941

to show that Germany would have been far better off without Italy as a partner. It was Italy's bungled campaigns in Greece and Albania, which Mussolini had thought would be a walk-over, that obliged Germany to send relieving forces to the Balkans. This proved a great strain on German resources and led to the dilution of her armies at critical times.

As fighting men, the Italian soldiers were as courageous as those of any other nation, but they were not well led or efficiently organized during the Second World War. On many occasions Germany forces had to be diverted to save Italian armies from defeat. This was the reason why Germany became involved in the North African desert campaigns that began in October 1940. Mussolini's aim was to aid the Axis war effort by seizing Egypt from Britain. Despite early successes for the Italian troops, their attempt to push the British forces out of Egypt failed. By early 1941, such was the Italian disarray that Germany had to come to its ally's assistance.

This marked the entry into the desert war of the Africa Corps under, arguably, Germany's most able commander, Irwin Rommel, who skilfully used his smaller army to inflict a number of damaging defeats on the British, including the capture of Tobruk in June 1941.

Germany declares war on the USA, December 1941

The conflict that had begun as a European war in September 1939 became a truly world war in December 1941, with the entry of Japan and the USA. Japan, as part of its strategy to gain a free hand in its control of East Asia, launched an intended knockout strike on the US Pacific Fleet at Pearl Harbor in Hawaii. However, the attack, far from forcing the USA out of the Pacific, did the very opposite. In declaring war on the Japanese empire, President Roosevelt, committed the American people to wage unceasing war until 'the day of infamy' had been avenged.

This marks the critical point where Germany under Hitler began to lose control over the military struggle which she had dominated up to then. The remarkable thing is that she could have avoided being drawn into the widening conflict. At this juncture, there was no need for Germany to become involved. It is true that a tri-partite pact between Italy, Germany and Japan had recently been signed, which committed each member to support the others should they go to war. But technically the agreement was not binding since Japan had failed to inform Germany of its intention to attack Pearl Harbor. However, although irritated that Japan had not consulted him, Hitler still decided that as an ally Germany would declare war on the United States. It was his personal decision. It was not forced upon him by circumstance.

What, then, led him to the momentous step of challenging the world's greatest military and economic power? The answer is that Hitler did not think the Americans would fight or, if they did, not for long. He was convinced that the anti-war mood that had been clearly evident in the USA between 1939 and 1941 meant that the Americans had no heart for the struggle. They would, therefore, soon be very willing to make a compromise peace with Germany and Japan which would leave both countries free to pursue their expansionist aims, Japan in Asia, Germany in Europe.

It proved to be a grave miscalculation. The Americans did not back off; they did the very reverse. They threw themselves into the struggle with a tremendous sense of commitment, pledging themselves to achieve total victory over the enemy. Moreover, in planning for the war, the USA under Roosevelt chose to make the defeat of Germany its strategic priority. That meant Germany would bear the full brunt of American arms. It can now be seen that Hitler's decision to take on the USA ranks alongside the attack on Russia before the Western Front had been closed, was one his greatest wartime errors. This was not immediately obvious but, with hindsight, it is clear that after December 1941, although Germany might not lose the war, it was very unlikely that she would win it.

05 Nazi Germany at war, 1942–5

This chapter will cover:

- how the tide of war turned against Germany
- the desert campaigns
- disaster on the Eastern Front
- the Allied invasion of Europe
- Hitler's last desperate gambles.

The position in 1942

The year 1942 marked the highest point in the fortunes of the Third Reich. Up to then it had suffered no major reverse. Save for the neutral countries, the whole of continental Europe from the Pyrenees to the Caucasus was either under direct German occupation or was subject to German control. Moscow and Leningrad were under siege, the desert war in North Africa under Rommel's direction was going decidedly Germany's way, and at sea the U-boats were enjoying marked success in the Atlantic struggle. Britain, it is true, remained undefeated, but her contribution to the continental war at this point was negligible. Although the USA had entered the war on the Allied side at the end of 1941, this seemed to be counterbalanced by Japan's joining the Axis powers as an active ally.

Ironically, it was Germany's earlier success that was to prove her undoing. She began to suffer from what economic historians call 'overstretch'. Spread across a vast area of Europe and North Africa, allied to an Italy that was beginning to prove more of a liability than an asset, confronted by the seemingly endless manpower of the Soviet Union and the massive economic resources of the USA, Germany in 1942 began to lose the initiative. From this stage on she was fighting an essentially defensive war.

The key moments and main phases of the war, 1942–5

1942	War in western desert
	Beginning of Battle of Stalingrad
	Allied victory at El Alamein
1943	German surrender at Stalingrad
	German defeat at Kursk
	Mussolini overthrown
	Italy switches to the Allied side
1944	Allied landings in Normandy open a second front in Western Europe
	Failure of July Bomb Plot to kill Hitler
	Battle of the Bulge
1945	Soviet forces take Berlin
	Hitler commits suicide
	Germany signs unconditional surrender

The desert war, 1942–3

Modern wars are invariably won by the side with superior resources. This was markedly true of the desert campaigns. The Afrika Korps' striking successes under Rommel in North Africa could not go on for ever. Rommel rarely received adequate reinforcements. This was partly because vital supply lines in the eastern Mediterranean were blocked by the British. It was also because Hitler, who regarded the desert war as no more than a holding operation, declined to provide Rommel with the supplies he desperately needed and continually requested. Rommel made superb use of his troops and equipment, but lack of materiel began to tell.

General Montgomery, his British counterpart, was not a spectacular commander but he was a great realist. He knew that if he could build up his Eighth Army's tanks and artillery he would eventually be able to overcome his more brilliant opponent. With dogged determination and patience, Montgomery waited until his army was overwhelmingly superior to Rommel's forces in troops and armaments. He then launched a massive assault. It was simple, even crude, but highly effective. In the Battle of El Alamein in October 1942 Rommel's army was defeated and forced to withdraw.

As it retreated westwards its path was blocked by an Anglo-American force under General Eisenhower, which had landed in Morocco and Algeria. Caught between the two Allied armies, Rommel put up a skilful resistance but was eventually overcome by greater numbers. In May 1943, over 300,000 German and Italian troops surrendered in Tunisia. This opened the way for Allied landings in southern Italy two months later, the first direct challenge to German control of Western Europe since 1939. The tide of the war had turned.

Both Hitler and Stalin dismissed the desert war as of minor importance. They were wrong. Hitler was of course angered by the Afrika Korps' ultimate failure. If he made light of it, it was only to avoid acknowledging the shame of defeat. Stalin sneered at the British successes in the desert because he claimed the real war was on the Eastern Front. In his view, the desert campaigns were Britain's way of pretending it was involved in a real anti-German struggle whereas its true aim was to see Germany and the USSR fight themselves to a standstill. Stalin claimed that was why the British delayed starting a second front on the European mainland until 1944.

But the desert was far from being a side-show. It influenced the overall war in three vital ways: it effectively destroyed the Italian war effort, showed that German armies could be beaten, and greatly lifted Allied morale.

The battle of Stalingrad, 1942–3

If the German loss at El Alamein was a disaster, then its defeat at Stalingrad on the Eastern Front four months later was a catastrophe. As part of their push south-eastward to seize the oil fields of the Caucasus, the German forces besieged the city of Stalingrad. The city was not of major strategic importance, but it bore Stalin's name. Defining it as a symbol of Russian resistance, Stalin demanded that his city be defended to the death. Hitler's response was perfectly matched. It was recorded in the official High Command report: 'The *Führer* orders that on entry into the city the entire male population be done away with.'

But, having entered Stalingrad, the Germans met such a ferocious resistance that they were forced onto the defensive. The besiegers became the besieged. Ignoring the appeals of his generals at the front, who urged a withdrawal, Hitler instructed his army to retreat not one millimetre. They were 'to fight to the last soldier and the last bullet.'

The result was that the German forces, deprived of supplies and reinforcements, were battered and starved into submission. Their surrender on 31 January 1943 was a blow from which Germany never recovered. As many as 200,000 German troops died in the battle. Another 91,000 became prisoners at its end; of these, only 6,000 would survive their captivity. The Sixth Army, which had been the most successful of all Germany's forces since the start of the war in 1939, had been destroyed.

Stalingrad was singly the most important conflict of the war in Europe. Its outcome destroyed the sense of invincibility in Hitler's armies and gave real promise of final victory to the Western Allies. The Soviet newspaper, *Red Star*, summed up the significance of it all:

> What was destroyed at Stalingrad was the flower of the German *Wehrmacht*. Hitler was particularly proud of the 6th Army and its great striking power. It was the first to invade Belgium. It took Paris. It took part in the invasion of Yugoslavia and Greece. Before the war it had taken

part in the occupation of Czechoslovakia. In 1942 it broke through from Karkov to Stalingrad. And now it does not exist.

(*Red Star*, 5 February 1943)

Hitler blamed the defeat on the large number of Romanian, Hungarian and Italian units fighting on the German side at Stalingrad. Had it been solely German troops engaged, as he claimed he had always wanted, there would have been no defeat. Yet it had been the German commander of the Sixth Army, von Paulus, whom Hitler had made Field Marshal in the belief that no one of such rank would dishonour himself by accepting defeat, who had personally delivered the surrender to the Russians. When he learned what von Paulus had done, Hitler screamed: 'How can someone be so cowardly? I don't understand it. So many people have to die. Then such a person goes and besmirches in the last minute the heroism of so many others.'

Germany fell into a deep melancholy. Troop losses on the scale of Stalingrad left millions of Germans bereaved. Mixed with their sorrow was an anger that they had been deceived for so long about the real character of the battle. It was only on the eve of defeat that the press and radio dropped their constant claims that a great victory was being won and admitted the truth. Although there were scattered protests, some of them aimed directly at the *Führer*, people's anger did not develop into an open challenge.

Yet there was a sense in which Stalingrad marked the point at which the special bond that Hitler had forged with the nation began to weaken. The apparatus of state control meant his authority would remain until the very last stage of the war, but the notion of Hitler as hero of his people had been irreparably damaged.

The battle of Kursk, July 1943

It was in an effort to regain his and his army's prestige in another part of the line that Hitler backed a plan proposed by Kurt Zeitzler, the General Chief of Staff. Zeitzler had noted that a large bulge had appeared where the Soviet forces had overextended their defensive line in the region of Kursk. He suggested that if the Germans were to launch a full-scale panzer attack they could break through the Soviet line and so regain the initiative on the Eastern Front.

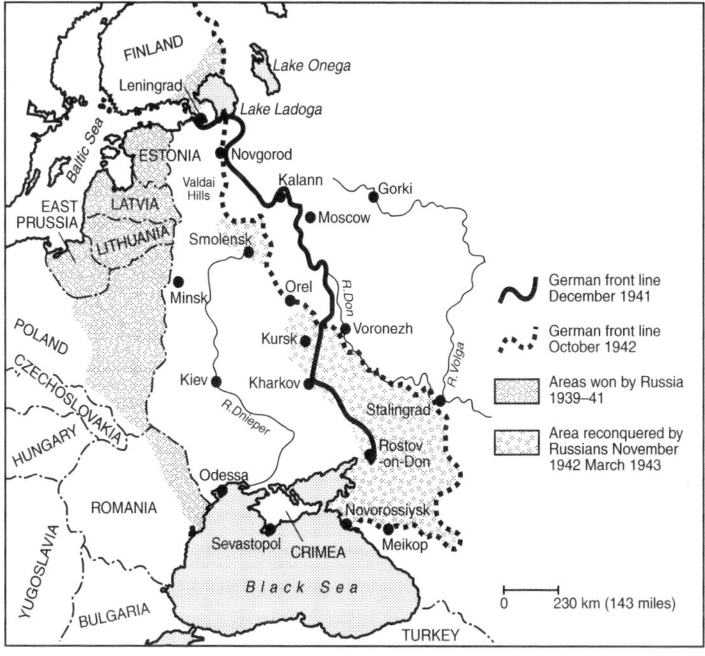

figure 8 map of the Eastern Front, 1939–43

So it was that on 5 July 1943 Operation Citadel was begun. It produced the largest tank battle in history. The Soviet commanders with astonishing speed poured their forces into the Kursk salient. Opposing the *Wehrmacht*'s 700,000 troops, 2,400 tanks, and 1,800 aircraft were the Soviet army's 1.3 million troops, 3,400 tanks and 2,100 aircraft. As had been the case in the western desert, it was numbers that mattered. After twelve days of savage attack and counter attack, the German forces still had not broken through. Mindful of Stalingrad, Hitler decided to save his armies from another devastating defeat by calling off the whole operation. The Soviet Union justifiably hailed it as another great victory. Kursk had confirmed what Stalingrad had revealed; the Soviet forces were winning the war in the East.

Crisis in Italy, 1943–5

These forebodings added to the grim news that Hitler had received two days before Citadel was unleashed; the British and the Americans had landed in Sicily, the toe of Italy. This was not the second front that Stalin had been demanding but it was the opening of another major campaign that would put increasing strain on Germany's ability to sustain the war. The truth was that her Axis ally, Italy, had become a huge burden. Hitler judged that Italian forces would not by themselves be capable of resisting the Allies. That is what helped persuade him to call off Citadel and transfer his Second Panzer division to Italy. He remarked that he regarded one German division as being worth 20 Italian ones.

Yet, whatever his dismissive view of Italy as a fighting force, he continued to have trust in its leader. In April 1943, he had gone to see Mussolini to assure him that, despite North Africa and Stalingrad, the Axis powers could still win the war. But the faith he had in Mussolini as an ally was destroyed by the events of late July. Mussolini was overthrown in an anti-fascist rising and arrested.

Within weeks the new Italian government under Marshal Badoglio made peace with the Allies and went over to their side. Hitler was now forced to occupy Italy as an enemy country and to commit huge numbers of German troops in an effort to prevent the Allied forces moving up from the south where they had landed after taking Sicily. Mussolini was rescued in a daring airborne raid by German paratroopers and installed as head of the Italian Social Republic, a vain attempt to give some form of legality to Germany's occupation of Italy.

Although Germany clung on to northern Italy until April 1945, it became an increasingly desperate and draining struggle. Hitler's involvement with his fellow fascist leader during the 12 years of the Third Reich was a remarkable story of misplaced belief in Italy's strength as an international power and misguided faith in Mussolini's value as a military ally. It was a story which brought Hitler little comfort.

Germany's troubles at sea and in the air, 1943–5

There is an interesting parallel between Germany's fortunes on land and at sea during the course of the war. The early years saw her do well in both areas. Admittedly, there were losses among her surface ships, the most dramatic being the sinking by the British in 1941 of the great battleship *Bismarck*. But Germany's skilful deployment of her submarine fleets made the crossing of the Atlantic a perilous affair for British convoys. The success of the U-boats threatened to starve Britain of food and materials.

Two key developments prevented this. One was the entry of the USA into the war with a determination to loosen Germany's naval stranglehold. The other was a remarkable technical development. British cryptologists at Bletchley Park perfected the Enigma decoding device which they used to decipher the Ultra system, Germany's method for sending secret messages which its encoders thought was so sophisticated as to be unbreakable. Provided with vital information concerning German naval movements, the Royal Navy was able to protect Allied convoys and take out many German vessels.

From 1943 the 'Battle of the Atlantic', as the war at sea was termed, coincided with the beginning of a sustained Anglo-American air offensive, which aimed to destroy Germany's economy. The Allied day and night raids were often costly in men and planes but they achieved the main objective of softening up Germany prior to a major land invasion. By 1944, Germany's air defences had practically ceased to exist. Devoid of fighter protection, German cities were subjected to a reign of terror from the skies.

In February 1945, the city of Dresden was blasted by RAF bombing raids. The intensity of the attacks caused a fire storm which killed 25,000 civilians and laid waste large areas of one of the most beautiful cities in Germany. Its devastation coming only three months before the end of the war was subsequently criticized as an unnecessary act of aggression. However, 60 years later it came to light from German sources that during the war Dresden had developed into a major industrial and communications centre. Over 125 factories concerned with war work were situated in and around the city. It was, therefore, a legitimate strategic target given the rules of engagement of the time. Goebbels's last great propaganda success was to portray the bombing of Dresden as an inhuman act. By a strange irony, his distorted portrayal remained, until very recently, the accepted version in Britain.

The Allied invasion of occupied Europe, 1944

By the summer of 1944, after months of preparation, the Allied forces were ready to open the long-awaited second front in Europe. On D-day, 6 June, British, American and Canadian troops stormed and took the Normandy beaches. They then began the process of pushing the German forces out of the occupied areas of Northern Europe. By September 1944, Paris and Brussels had been liberated. Germany itself was now under threat.

Hitler's last throw – the V weapons, 1944–5

The Normandy landings coincided with what proved to be Hitler's last throw of the dice – his use of terror weapons against Britain. The attacks by the V1 flying bomb (a pilotless jet-propelled plane loaded with explosives), which began in June, were followed in September by the launching of the V2 (an armed rocket). Hitler hoped the havoc they would cause would force the Allies to call off their air raids on Germany and perhaps even withdraw their forces from Europe. These seem wild dreams now, but had the V weapons struck in the numbers intended the devastation might have become unbearable and Britain might have considered a compromise peace with Germany.

But these are speculations. What actually happened was that the weapons caused widespread death and damage in and around London and led to the evacuation of one and a half million people. However, owing to Allied bombing of the launch sites and later the overrunning of them by Allied land forces, the destruction was never on the scale Hitler had originally planned. His last effort to turn the tide of the war by terrorizing Britain's civilian population had failed.

The end for Germany and Hitler, 1945

The Germans fought on courageously, but they were now caught in a closing three-pronged claw made up of the Allied armies advancing eastward towards the Rhine, pushing up through Italy towards southern Germany, with Soviet armies

V1 Flying bomb attacks

Number of V1s fired – 10,000

3,676 hit London

2,600 failed to reach their target

1,878 were shot down by anti-air batteries

1,846 were destroyed by fighters

Number of people killed by the V1s – 6,184

Number of V2s launched – 1,115

Number of people killed – 2,754

moving westwards into Germany on a series of fronts. After one last desperate resistance in the Battle of the Bulge in the Ardennes in early 1945, Germany had nothing left. The grim figures are that, between September 1939 and September 1944, 2.8 million Germans were killed; in the succeeding nine months, up to the surrender in May 1945, the death toll was 4.8 million.

By the end of 1944, Hitler was a sick man. Some observers said he never really recovered from the attempt on his life in the July Bomb Plot (see page 169). He had aged prematurely and had begun to develop the twitching symptoms of Parkinson's disease. He no longer appeared in public and addressed the people on only two occasions on radio during the last year of his life. He seemed to have lost the gift of leadership. His authority was now based on terror not inspiration.

By now the mass of the German population no longer believed they could win the war. There was a common saying among them that, grim though defeat might be, it was better to face 'an end with horror than continue with a horror without end.' It required ever restrictive measures to keep the people in line. Hitler gave Himmler's SS complete freedom to act as ruthlessly as it saw fit against 'saboteurs and traitors', terms that could be used against anyone who expressed defeatist ideas.

But coercion could not save Germany. By April the position was totally hopeless. To avoid capture by the Russians who had entered Berlin, Hitler committed suicide on 30 April in his Berlin bunker. On 7 May the German government agreed to an unconditional surrender. The Third Reich was no more.

06 the Nazi leaders

This chapter will cover:

- the principal figures in the Third Reich
- their background
- their role in Nazi Germany
- their eventual fate.

There was never a formal list of who was in government under Hitler. Ministers fell in and out of favour and his was always the final voice in any disputed decision. The following is a list of those Nazis who merit special attention because of their closeness to the *Führer* or the important role they played in the running of Nazi Germany.

Martin Bormann (1900–45)

As Nazi-Party Secretary, Bormann became the confidant of the *Führer*; during the war he was increasingly responsible for conveying Hitler's instructions to the Party and to ministers and officials. After Rudolf Hess's flight to Britain in 1941 (see page 63), Bormann was Hitler's right-hand man. Although Bormann was an able administrator, he was disliked by many in the party and found his policies obstructed by opponents. However, his closeness to the *Führer* saved him from open challenge.

Bormann became notorious for his savage anti-Semitism. In 1942, he ordered that ruthless force be used to achieve 'the permanent elimination of the Jews from the territories of Greater Germany'. As a committed atheist, he also launched a fierce attack on the churches in Germany, arguing that their power 'must absolutely and finally be broken'. In the confused last days of the Third Reich, Bormann came to regard himself as Hitler's successor. There is considerable uncertainty about his eventual fate. One story is that, rather than fall into Russian hands, he committed suicide in Berlin in May 1945. Another suggestion is that he escaped to South America where he remained until his death in 1973.

Joseph Goebbels (1897–1945)

Goebbels was born into a respectable Catholic family in the northern Rhineland. Throughout his life he kept a diary. In its pages can be traced the development of perhaps the most intellectually gifted of the Nazi leaders. He was a very able student and gained a doctorate in philosophy at Heidelberg University. But if nature had given him a good mind it seemed to compensate by leaving him physically disabled. He was short and cursed with a club foot which left him with a pronounced limp and an inferiority complex. As a child he was ribbed mercilessly over his small size and his lameness. He had pretensions as a writer but could not find a publisher for his works. In his diary he wrote self-pityingly, 'Why does fate deny to me what it gives to others?'

Goebbels's early political thinking drew him to Communism. He was impressed by its party discipline and sense of historical purpose. This was why the socialist aspect of National Socialism appealed to him the more. However, once he had come under Hitler's spell by 1926, he transferred his commitment to Nazism with its emphasis on nationalism and race. He outmanoeuvred his challengers in the Party and won Hitler's confidence. Of all the prominent Nazis, Goebbels had the most genuine affection for Hitler. Unlike Rudolf Hess, who had a dog-like devotion to the *Führer*, Goebbels from the beginning tried to rationalize his affection. In 1925 he wrote in his journal, 'Adolf Hitler I love you because you are both great and simple at the same time – what one calls a genius.'

The admiration, if not the adulation, was two-way. Hitler saw in Goebbels a person of great potential and organizing ability and, soon after taking power in 1933, appointed him Minister of Enlightenment and Propaganda. Both men were apparently unaware of the ironic contradiction in the title of the office.

Goebbels became increasingly committed to the *Führer* after the war turned against Germany in 1943. It was Goebbels who led the call for total war after the defeat at Stalingrad. In his increasingly fanatical speeches he demanded that Germans expose the backsliders and defeatists amongst the population. Even when the situation had become hopeless, he rejected any suggestion of suing for peace. He continued to demand absolute obedience and dedication to the Nazi cause. At the end, in Hitler's Berlin bunker his fanaticism turned into a death wish. He shared with Hitler the belief that it was better for Germany to be destroyed than to surrender. He personalized this in a final desperate act by inducing his wife to die with him in a suicide pact and by killing his children.

Hermann Goering (1893–1945)

Second only to Hitler in the Third Reich's pecking order, Goering was in many ways the most interesting of the Nazi leaders. Born into a prosperous Prussian family in the diplomatic service, he tended to despise the coarser Nazi members who lacked the sophistication that he claimed. A darling of the ladies, Goering, before he ran to fat, was a handsome young man who had gained a deserved reputation for bravery as a flying ace in the First World War. He developed his politics in Prussia where he helped organize a fierce anti-Communist repression. He served as Prussian deputy in the Reichstag. Driven by a powerful sense of ambition, Goering's main aim was always to further his own position. He joined the Nazi Party in 1923 and was at Hitler's side during the failed putsch in Munich in that year. He was made President of the Reichstag in 1933.

Goering earned Hitler's gratitude by playing a major role in the destruction of Röhm and the SA in 1934. As Reich Air Minister from 1934 on, his greatest, though eventually fatally flawed, achievement was the creation of the *Luftwaffe*, the German Air Force. Despite its successes in the early part of the war with its *Blitzkrieg* tactics, it proved ultimately incapable of making a decisive contribution to the war on the Russian front and was unable to defend Germany against the blanket bombing of the Allies during the last stages of the war.

Goering's vanity and greed became legendary. During his time as 'Plenipotentiary' for the Four Year Economic Plan, which he introduced in 1936, he named a giant industrial plant after himself – 'the Hermann Goering Works'. A joke heard in Britain was to follow this title with the question – 'Yes, but what at?' It was during the period he was responsible for economic planning that he amassed a huge fortune for himself through his contacts with big business. I. G. Farben and Siemens were among the leading companies from whom he received large under-the-counter payments for his help in obtaining contracts for them.

Goering also involved himself in the diplomacy of the Third Reich. During the *Anschluss* crisis in 1938 he guided Seyss-Inquart and the Austrian Nazis in pressing their claims for incorporation within the Third Reich. He also had *Luftwaffe* planes waiting at frontier airstrips in case force was needed. In the same year, it was Goering who drafted the agreement on which the Munich settlement was based. Such was his keenness to interfere in foreign affairs that he often fell out with the Foreign Secretary Ribbentrop, a man for whom Goering developed a powerful distaste.

As with nearly all the Nazis, Goering was fiercely and actively anti-Semitic. In the aftermath of *Kristallnacht* (literally, 'the night of glass', a reference to the smashing of Jewish property and synagogues) in 1938, he ordered that the Jewish community be fined one million marks and be debarred from playing any part in the German economy. In July 1941, he instructed Reinhard Heydrich 'to carry out all preparations with regard to a general solution of the Jewish question in all those territories of Europe which are under German influence.' It was this order that led to the Wannsee conference of 1942, which began the planning of the Final Solution (see page 138).

Renowned, even notorious, for his lavish playboy lifestyle, he described himself as 'the last Renaissance man'. He loved to show off his private collection of priceless paintings and fine art, most of it stolen from German Jews or seized in the occupied countries. Goering was known to have received guests in his luxury Berlin flat dressed in a voluminous red caftan and presenting himself as a Turkish Sultan. He sometimes changed his uniforms and outfits five or six times a day.

His often outrageous behaviour helps to explain why he was perhaps the most popular of the Nazi leaders. Hitler was revered, worshipped even, but his arid private life was not something ordinary Germans could identify with easily. But Goering's high living, while it may have been frowned upon in official circles, made him appear very human and endeared him to many Germans.

In the largely meaningless political manoeuvrings that took place during the final stages of the war as the Third Reich collapsed, Hitler lost all faith in Goering. He removed him as Deputy *Führer*, replacing him with Martin Bormann. When Goering tried a coup of his own, he was expelled from the Nazi Party, but by then it hardly mattered.

At his trial in November 1946, following his capture by the Americans, Goering appeared truculent and unrepentant, but he did defend himself with considerable skill. He claimed he was no more guilty of war crimes than the Allied leaders, and told the court that he was being tried only because Germany had lost the war. Nevertheless, he was sentenced to death. Two hours before he was due to be hanged, he committed suicide by chewing on a glass phial of prussic acid that he had secreted in his mouth.

Rudolf Hess (1894–1987)

On the night of 10 May 1941, a lone Messerschmitt 110 crashed in flames in the Scottish lowlands not far from Glasgow. Just before the plane began its last dive, observers saw the pilot bale out. It was the first jump the parachutist had ever made; he landed awkwardly injuring his leg. In a mixture of German and English he told the locals who ran up to him that his name was Alfred Horn, and he wished to be taken to the Duke of Hamilton.

But he was not Herr Horn; he was Rudolf Hess, deputy *Führer* of the Third Reich. His bizarre journey had been undertaken entirely on his own initiative. Without informing anyone, Hess had flown to Britain with the intention of asking the Duke of Hamilton, an RAF officer, to liaise with the British government with a view to starting Anglo-German peace talks. Hess had left a letter in Germany explaining his reasons. This was duly read out to Hitler when news of the remarkable escapade reached the Berghof, the *Führer*'s residence in Bavaria. In his letter, Hess stated that his chief aim was to start negotiations that would bring about an end to the war between Germany and Britain so that that they would be allies not enemies when the imminent attack on Russia began.

Hitler became apoplectic with rage. One of his first reactions was to abolish the office of Deputy Leader of the Party and to appoint Martin Bormann as the head of a newly created Party Chancellery. Over the radio it was formally announced in pitying rather than angry tones that Rudolf Hess had succumbed to 'confusion and mental derangement'. In private, Goebbels expressed the embarrassment of the government and party by pointedly asking, 'How could such an idiot be the second man after the *Führer*?' It was a good question. The Hess extravaganza revealed that the Third Reich, for all its array of power and all its claims to a providential destiny as the saviour of the Aryan race, was being run by men with brittle and disordered minds.

Hess was, indeed, a very odd man. He may even have been clinically insane, though this was not necessarily a handicap in the Nazi movement. Having fought as an infantry soldier and as a pilot in the First World War, he was embittered by Germany's surrender in 1918. Drawn to nationalist politics, he met Hitler in 1920 and became his political secretary. He took part in the Munich putsch in 1923 and was imprisoned along with Hitler. It was during their time together in Landsberg fortress that, Hess said, he became convinced of 'the mighty significance' of Adolf Hitler. It was to Hess that Hitler dictated the first draft of *Mein Kampf*.

From then on he was a fawning admirer of his leader. He heaped praise on him and delivered such cringe-making speeches at party rallies that they came close to embarrassing Hitler himself. At the time of the Night of the Long Knives, Hess said he himself would have loved to have shot Röhm. His sycophancy earned him the deputy leadership of the Nazi Party in 1934, and in 1939 he was nominated as next in line, after Goering, to Hitler as head of state. Such elevation may have finally unhinged Hess's already disturbed personality.

The madcap venture that took him to Scotland came to nothing. His overtures were taken up by neither the British nor German governments. He was held captive in Britain for the rest of the war. In 1946, Hess appeared before the Nuremberg tribunal and was sentenced to life imprisonment, a term which he fully served before dying, the only prisoner left in Spandau gaol, in 1987 at the age of 93. He had outlived all the other Nazi leaders.

Reinhard Heydrich (1904–42)

Heydrich, born the son of a music teacher, had been an active member of the *Freikorps* which he joined in 1919 at the age of 15. He was attracted by the racial theories of the Nazis and offered his services to the movement. After a period in the navy, from which he was dismissed in 1931 for 'conduct unbecoming' with the daughter of a shipyard owner, he made a rapid rise up the Nazi hierarchy. He became second-in-command to Himmler, the SS leader, and then became head of the SD (intelligence service) in his own right. He won Hitler's admiration by playing an important part in preparing the attack on the SA in the Night of the Long Knives episode in 1934.

Possessed of a very sharp mind, Heydrich despised the oafishness and stupidity that characterized so many of the Nazis. Yet the perverted use to which he put his intellectual gifts makes him one of the most repugnant of the high-ranking Nazis. It was he who dreamed up the idea of making the Jews wear yellow stars. Regarded as physically handsome and renowned as a ladies' man, he was a moral degenerate who delighted in terror. As head of the Berlin Gestapo he told his officers in 1934:

> The Jews' possibilities for living are to be curtailed, and not simply in an economic sense. Germany must be for them a country without future, in which the residual older generations can certainly die, but in which the

young cannot live. One does not fight rats with a revolver, but rather with poison and gas.

The reference to killing vermin with poison and gas has a fearful prophetic resonance. It would be these very methods that would be employed to murder the Jews when the 'Final Solution' was adopted less than a decade later. Heydrich was to be a major figure in this. At the infamous Wannsee conference in January 1942, it was he who drafted the Protocol, the document that laid down the strategy for the extermination of the Jewish race in Europe. There is a curious psychological aspect to all this. It was often rumoured that despite his blonde hair and blue eyes, which made him appear the perfect Nordic type, Heydrich was in fact of Jewish stock. His virulent hatred of the Jews may, therefore, have been a product of self-loathing.

As head of the Reich security system after 1936, Heydrich proved himself a very skilful but ruthless gatherer of information, not only on suspected 'enemies of the State' but also on members of the Party and government. This made him enemies within the Nazi movement, but he revelled in the pitiless world of power politics, no matter whether this was engaging in espionage abroad or intrigue at home.

In 1941, at the age of 37, he was appointed 'Protector' of Bohemia and Moravia, where his vicious treatment of the Czech people earned him the nick-name of 'butcher Heydrich'. Such was his driving sense of personal ambition that it was widely rumoured that he coveted Hitler's position as *Führer*. But how high Heydrich might have risen became an academic question after he was assassinated in Prague in May 1942. Two Czech partisans, who had been specially trained in Britain and parachuted in, ambushed his car and shot him. Although Heydrich's wounds were only minor, complications set in and he died in great agony from blood poisoning. Perhaps there is a God after all.

Tragically for the Czech people, his death led to the most fearful reprisals. Repression was intensified. Over 1,200 Czechs were murdered and, in one of the most despicable acts committed by a despicable regime, the village of Lidice was destroyed. On the pretext that one of the resistance fighters had connections with Lidice, the village was chosen for exemplary retribution. Its buildings were razed, its men publicly executed, its women transported to Ravensbruck concentration camp, and its children sent to Germany to be experimented on. The village has been preserved in its devastated state as a memorial to the dead and a reminder of the horrors that took place there.

Heinrich Himmler (1900–45)

In the rogue's gallery of Nazism, one of the most unattractive exhibits was Heinrich Himmler. His bullet head and brutal haircut somehow expressed his character in ways that he could not have intended. He was the archetypal bureaucrat, capable of working 18 hours a day and appearing to enjoy it. He had seen more of the open air in his younger days when he had worked as a poultry farmer after military service during the First World War.

Himmler had been born into a Catholic family in Munich, where his father was a schoolmaster. By 1925 he had joined the Nazi Party. His taste for organization and administration led Hitler to appoint him head of his SS bodyguard in 1929. From that position he rose to become chief of the Prussian Gestapo in 1934. Two years later he was placed in command of all the Gestapo forces in Germany. Towards the end of the war, he became Minister of the Interior and Commander-in-Chief of the home forces.

Himmler more than anyone was responsible for the brutal concentration-camp system being maintained and extended. On his visits to these camps he seemed at times to be disturbed by the atrocious conditions he saw but this never lessened his aim of turning them into mass extermination centres. He gave a clue to his feelings when he told a group of SS commandants in 1943 that though they were engaged in fearful activities that ordinary Germans would have been repelled by, it was necessary that they carry on their truly heroic work for the sake of the Fatherland. They had created 'a glorious page in our history, and one that has never been written and never can be written. We had the moral right, we had the duty to our people, to destroy this people which wanted to destroy us.'

Himmler was captured by British forces late in May 1945. He was wearing the uniform of an army sergeant. Rather than wait to be tried, he killed himself in his cell by swallowing cyanide, thus joining the ranks of all those Nazi leaders who thought it better to take their own life than suffer execution at the hands of the victors.

Albert Speer (1905–81)

If anyone qualifies for the title, 'the good Nazi', the strongest claimant would be Albert Speer. Of all the leaders who were arrested and put on trial at Nuremberg, Speer was the only one to show genuine remorse. He regretted what he had been involved in and what he had done. After his release from life imprisonment, he continued to accept his guilt and, insofar as he could, he made reparation for his membership of what he acknowledged had been a monstrous regime.

Speer rose to prominence and came to Hitler's attention as a bright young architect. Hitler had grandiose schemes for rebuilding Germany's cities. The capital Berlin became a centrepiece. Speer designed a whole series of models that delighted the *Führer*. Grandness of scale was the characteristic. Speer also played a significant role in preparing the Nuremberg rallies. He developed dramatic ways to illuminate the buildings and the massed Nazi ranks with sweeping search lights and flares. But he was often exasperated by the failure of the older Nazis, the heroes of the putsch and the street fighting, to form neat lines because their bulging beer guts spoiled the symmetry.

Speer went on to become a leading economic planner. Supported by Hitler, who took a strong personal liking to him, Speer became Minister of Munitions in 1942. He set about streamlining the system of industrial production, calling on the expertise of the major industrialists. Between 1942 and 1944 he worked wonders in raising armaments production at a time when Germany began to suffer military reverses and heavy bombing for the first time.

That the German economy never became the full war economy that Hitler had hoped for was not Speer's fault. Although he had wide-ranging powers, he was unable in the short time available to him as Economics Minister to overcome the vested interest of local officials and rival Nazi ministries who often dragged their feet in order to protect their own particular interests.

When Claus von Stauffenberg was preparing his assassination attempt in 1944, he met Hitler and a group of his closest ministers. Stauffenberg noted that Hitler was a trembling wreck, Goering was wearing heavy make-up, and Goebbels grinned like an idiot. He concluded that Speer was the only sane man present. Speer himself later admitted that Hitler had been, 'a truly satanic figure, presiding over a devil's court.' Although

Speer grew increasingly disillusioned as the war situation worsened, he never openly turned against his *Führer*. At the time of the July Bomb Plot, he worked closely with Goebbels to crush the possibility of an armed rising. It is true that he declined to carry out fully Hitler's orders to implement 'a scorched earth policy', that is to destroy anything in the whole of German industry that might fall into enemy hands. But there have been suggestions that Speer may possibly have had an eye to the future; realizing the cause was lost and that he would doubtless be called to account if he were taken prisoner, Speer wanted to show the Allies that he had not been amongst the most barbarous members of Hitler's regime.

Joachim von Ribbentrop (1893–1946)

Ribbentrop was a vain man with pretensions to grandeur. He made play of the 'von' in his name, claiming it was evidence of his aristocratic lineage. Service as a cavalry officer was followed by a period as a wine salesman. He travelled widely and became an accomplished linguist. In a smart career move, he boosted his social and financial standing by marrying the heiress to the hugely prosperous Henckel manufacturing family.

He did not join the Nazi Party until 1932. His lack of a sense of humour and his aloof manner made him unpopular with Party members, but there was no denying his commitment to the Nazi cause. His specialism was foreign intelligence gathering. By 1936 had he established a successful department which provided Hitler with highly useful information on foreign affairs. After being German Ambassador in Britain between 1936 and 1938, he returned to Berlin to become Foreign Minister, a post he held until the collapse of the Third Reich in 1945.

Ribbentrop may have put on airs and given the impression that he was making German foreign policy, but the truth is he was really Hitler's cipher. It was the *Führer* who laid down policy, Ribbentrop who conducted it. That is what gave the aggressive character to Ribbentrop's style. He was carrying out the *Führer*'s commands and this reflected itself in his uncompromising approach. British diplomats found in the 1930s how rigid Ribbentrop could be when defending Germany's interests as defined by Hitler.

At his trial at Nuremberg, Ribbentrop was charged with having been an aggressive warmonger. The charge was a fair one. Rarely did Ribbentrop attempt to challenge Hitler's ideas. The only influence he exerted was in reinforcing the *Führer*'s views, not in opposing them. That is why he and Goering had very strained relations. Goering, who believed that war with Britain was avoidable, blamed Ribbentrop for failing to warn Hitler that Britain was prepared to fight over Poland.

At the time, however, such criticisms of Ribbentrop meant little in the face of what appeared to be his brilliant diplomatic manoeuvring in achieving the Nazi-Soviet Pact of August 1939. This was followed in the September of the following year by another diplomatic coup, the signing of the Tripartite Pact, by which Germany, Italy and Japan agreed to come to each other's aid should one of them be attacked by another power. By March 1941, Hungary, Romania, Slovakia, Bulgaria and Yugoslavia had joined the Pact. With Britain seemingly on the verge of collapse and Western Europe under German control, the Pact could be seen as the climax of a dizzyingly successful period in the expansion of Nazi Germany.

This success appeared to lose some of its edge when, under the terms of the Pact, Germany was drawn into war with the USA following the Japanese attack on the American fleet in Pearl Harbor in December 1941. But, at the time, it was not realized that Hitler's personal decision to take on the Americans would involve Germany in a four-year struggle with the greatest power on earth, a struggle which Germany could not win. Despite things turning against Germany from 1942 on, Ribbentrop never lost his faith in Hitler's judgement.

Arrested at the close of the war, he was found guilty at Nuremberg of war crimes and hanged in October 1946. Observers said Ribbentrop derived a perverse pleasure from the knowledge that Goering's suicide two hours before the executions were due to begin meant he himself would now be the first of the Nazi leaders to be hanged.

Alfred Rosenberg (1893–1946)

A German from Latvia, Rosenberg was sometimes referred to as the Party's 'philosopher'. A member of the Nazi Party from its earliest days, he developed a series of theories extolling the virtues of the Aryan race and warning against the pollution of it by Jewish blood. He was as virulent in his anti-Semitism as Hitler. The bitter irony of this was that Rosenberg's name and physical appearance suggested that he was of Jewish stock himself.

In 1934, he was put in charge of the Third Reich's cultural and educational policies. When he was appointed Minister for the Occupied East in April 1941, he set about turning his racial hatreds into a systematic extermination programme. He drafted schemes for subdividing Eastern Europe and Russia into a set of satellite states whose people would be worked to death in order to provide goods and materials for greater Germany. It was for these crimes that he was hanged at Nuremberg in 1946.

The Nazi leaders in history

An extraordinary feature of Nazi Germany is how far short of Aryan perfection most of its leaders fell. Hitler himself was short in stature and suffered from gum disease which left him with permanently foul breath. There was something essentially ridiculous about him, as Charlie Chaplin brilliantly captured in his thinly disguised portrayal of him in the film, *The Great Dictator* (1940). Goebbels was a club-footed diminutive, as gifted as Hitler as a rabble-rousing orator, but always conscious of how physically unprepossessing he was. Goering had been handsome in his youth but by the time the Third Reich came into being he was a bloated caricature of his former self, struggling not to burst out of the extra large uniforms specially tailored for him. Himmler was a dull, short-sighted bureaucrat, the personification of tedium, who actually enjoyed sitting at his desk 18 hours a day churning out orders and reports. Hess was so mad that even his fellow Nazis noticed.

Had the times not been so unstable in Germany these men would have remained a bunch of emotionally crippled misfits, impotently acting out their delusions on the fringe of politics. But, by a cruel historical irony, the tumultuous era they lived in allowed them to take power and work their disastrous ideas upon Germany and Europe.

the German economy under the Nazis

This chapter will cover:

- Hitler's economic priorities
- the role of Schacht, Goering and Speer as economic planners
- the importance of the Four Year Plan
- the impact of war on the economy.

Hitler's economic aims

Historians have often remarked that Hitler was a lucky politician. He was certainly lucky in regard to economics, at least in peacetime. The 1930s were a period of international recovery from economic depression, and Germany shared in that recovery. This gave Hitler a reputation for having created a powerful industry, which had ended unemployment and restored Germany's pride in herself. But while it is true that Germany did perform well down to 1939, Hitler's aim was not economic growth for its own sake. He was less concerned with improving the living standards of the people – though that did happen in peacetime – than with creating a strong industrial economy that would provide the sinews of war. Hitler was not himself an economic planner. He left that to his economics ministers and gave them considerable freedom to get on with the job. But his demand was that they prepare Germany for rearmament. That was their prime task and duty.

The development of the German economy under Hitler, therefore, is a story of a series of strategies followed by a succession of ministers, trying in often quite different ways to meet Hitler's wishes. There was no single, consistent Nazi economic programme or master plan. The economy of the Third Reich juddered on in fits and starts. The first stage was associated very closely with the work of Hjalmar Schacht.

The policies of Hjalmar Schacht, 1933

Schacht had been brought up in the United Sates but returned to Germany to take a doctorate in economics at Berlin University. His exotic full name was Hjalmar Horace Greeley Schacht, his family having given him his middle names after a 19th century American journalist they admired. Schacht never became a Nazi party member. This made him distrusted in the eyes of some, such as Goering. But there was no doubting his ability as a financier and economist. He had played a principal part in stabilizing the German currency and ending the catastrophic inflation that had struck Germany in 1923.

It was also the case that he despised the weakness of the Weimar Republic and saw in Hitler someone who, despite his extreme political ideas, could make Germany powerful again. Schacht remarked, 'I desire a great and strong Germany and to achieve it I would enter an alliance with the devil.' That was why he helped form the Harzburg Front and persuaded the major industrial companies, for example, Krupp Steel and I. G. Farben, the chemical giants, to support the Nazis in the elections of the early 1930s. He also urged Hindenburg to make Hitler Chancellor.

Schacht's reward for this was his appointment as President of the Reichsbank in 1933 and Economics Minister in the following year. His plan for the recovery of the German economy was complex in detail but simple in its basic aim. Since Hitler gave him an almost entirely free hand at first, Schacht could develop his plans without interference. This appropriately matched his belief in the free market, the notion that financiers and businessmen should be able to get on with what they did best without direction from above by the government. He did not want the Nazi Party to take over the economy and dictate to Germany's business world what it should be doing. Using his many contacts among the big bankers and industrialists, Schacht established the Organization of Industry. This was a body made up of business guilds, employers' associations and finance houses.

So successful was the Organization in promoting trade and industry that a number of countries began to advance loans to Germany. This was a remarkable achievement for a country which since 1918 had struggled desperately to raise capital for itself. Schacht also approved of taxation as a way of increasing state funds. However, he insisted on two things: tax should be fairly assessed so that it would not be a burden and disincentive to private industry, and the revenue that it brought in should not be wasted but reinvested by the government in productive ways.

Aware that the bitterness created by high unemployment had been a major factor in the rise of the Nazis and that, therefore, they would be expected to tackle it, Schacht turned his attention to that. In 1934, he introduced the 'New Plan'. This was a set of measures for creating employment through public works schemes, such as road repairs, forest clearing and planting, and the building of new hospitals and schools. Young men aged 18–25 were required to join the National Labour Service for six months, during which time they would be trained in basic skills and directed to work where it was most needed.

Since Hitler's main objective was the expansion of Germany's military strength, Schacht knew that as Economics Minister he would have to consider plans for rearmament. But he did not want spending on arms to undermine economic recovery by draining away vital funds. He therefore proposed that rearmament be carefully planned and costed, and introduced in stages as the economy grew stronger. But this was too slow and unambitious for the Nazis. Hitler let it be known that he was becoming impatient with Schacht. A *Führer* memorandum of August 1936 asserted: 'If we do not succeed in bringing the German Army as rapidly as possible to the rank of the premier army in the world then Germany will be lost.' Schacht was not dismissed but he was bypassed. His adversary, Hermann Goering, was given the task of pushing Germany towards rapid militarization.

Goering's Four Year Plan, 1936–9

Goering's first move was to introduce a Four Year Plan in October 1936.

The chief aim was to make Germany an autarky; that is to say, an economically self-sufficient and self-governing power. To achieve this, a number of targets were set. The principal ones were the bringing of Germany's labour force under tighter control so that it could be directed into vital areas such as arms production, the use of import controls to protect German manufactures, and the rapid production of synthetic substitutes for rubber and oil so that these necessities would not have to be bought expensively from abroad. Agricultural growth was also included in the plan, but it was not given priority. Food consumption was not as important as arms production.

With more than a hint of self-mockery, the corpulent Goering remarked, 'guns will make us strong, butter will make us fat'.

The Four Year Plan had been intended to put the German economy on a war footing. Yet when war came in 1939, Germany was three years short of being ready for the struggle that followed. Goering was later blamed for this. Schacht described him as being a mere amateur in economics who was saved from the consequences of his bungling and incompetence only by Hitler's unshakeable faith in him.

Most economic historians suggest that by the 20th century autarky was an impossible goal for advanced industrial states like Germany. Their economies were too interlinked internationally. In 1939, German industry was still importing a third of the raw materials it needed. Nevertheless, although autarky had clearly not been achieved by that date, Germany had made significant economic advances which were the result of both Schacht's more subtle policies and the Four Year Plan's more aggressive ones.

	Consumer goods	Industrial goods
1933	80	56
1934	91	81
1936	100	114
1938	116	144

table 2 the growth in German manufactures (calculated to an index of 100 in 1928)

	Britain	Germany
1935	2%	8%
1936	5%	13%
1937	7%	13%
1938	8%	17%
1939	22%	23%

table 3 Germany's spending on arms compared with Britain's (calculated as a percentage of Gross National Product)

1928	125
1933	88
1934	94
1936	100
1938	106

table 4 The rise in wages of the average German industrial worker (calculated to an index of 100 in 1936)

The most striking aspect of Germany's economic performance was the sustained fall in unemployment. This suggested that Hitler's government had been a success and added greatly to his popularity. While the increase in employment may have owed much to the recovery of the world economy generally, the fact was that in the 1930s no industrial country in Europe or, indeed, in North America, could boast such impressive figures.

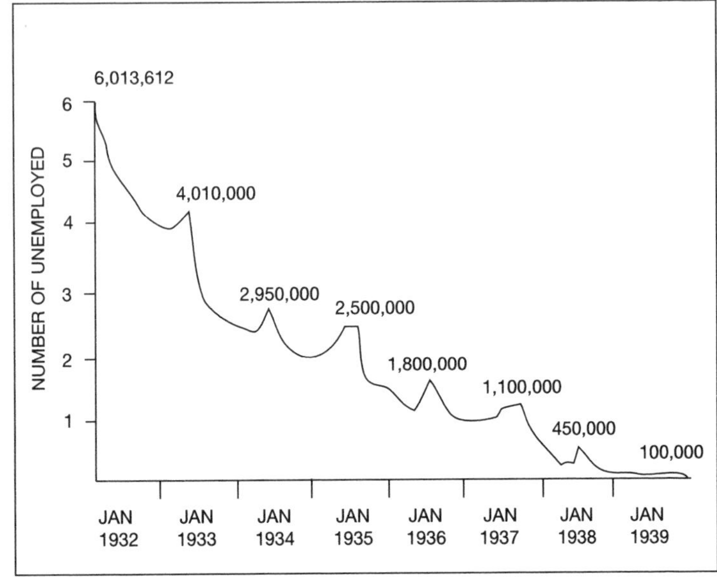

figure 9 graph showing the fall in unemployment in Germany, 1932–9

The economy in wartime, 1939–42

The great test of any economy is how well it copes with the demands of war. Schacht believed that Germany was not strong enough to sustain a major war. From 1939, when he stood down from his post as head of the Reichsbank, he became increasingly convinced that Nazi policies were leading Germany towards destruction. His sympathies were with the resistance groups, though he did not join in any of the assassination plans. Nevertheless, he was arrested after the July Bomb Plot in 1944 and sent to a concentration camp. He survived this, as he also did being held by the Americans in 1945 as a suspected war criminal. Eventually cleared of all charges, he went on to build a second highly successful career as a businessman in post-war Germany.

By 1938, Schacht's views were largely disregarded by Hitler, who was now set on expansion and who announced major spending programmes for all three services in July. These would make Germany ready for war. But which war? What Hitler had in mind was war in the East, the takeover of Czechoslovakia and Poland. He did not at this stage envisage war in Western Europe. To be ready for that would take Germany another four years, he calculated. He had grounds for regarding this as a logical policy. The Munich agreement in September 1938 confirmed his judgement that the Western Allies were not prepared to fight. His plans, therefore, were all to do with German expansion eastwards. By his reckoning, the rearmament programme that Germany was following would be adequate to sustain the effort involved.

However, when war came against Britain and France in the autumn of 1939, it was not the war that Hitler had prepared for. German military planning was far from complete. It was reckoned that Germany needed another three years of growth and rearmament to achieve military superiority in Europe. It was their awareness of this that concerned a number of his generals who thought that Hitler had gone too far too soon. Their worries deepened when they learned that Germany would be on her own – Mussolini had announced in August that Italy was not yet in a position to go to war as an ally of Germany.

Although both the German and the Allied commanders overestimated the strength of their opponents' military resources, the Germans were quite right in thinking that they were outmatched by the combined forces of France and Britain. As Table 5 shows, it was only in numbers of military aircraft that Germany was dominant. These details were not, of course, known at the time. Britain and France tended to think that German was stronger because that is what Hitler kept telling them. The confident warlike tone of his speeches convinced the Allies that what he was saying was true. It was very effective propaganda.

	Germany	France	Britain	Poland	Italy
Population	68 m	41.6 m	47.7 m	34.6 m	43.8 m
Size of armies	800,000	800,000	220,000	290,000	800,000
Military aircraft	4,500	600	2,075	390	1,500
Surface warships	17	28	184	4	60
Submarines	56	70	58	5	100
(m= million)					

table 5 The relative strength of the Axis powers and the Allies in September 1939

In the event, the German army's brilliant successes during the eight months between the defeat of Poland and the fall of France wiped away German self-doubting. Being an opportunist, Hitler quickly adapted to the situation, assuring his people that all had been well all along.

It might be thought that, with the sweeping German victories across Western Europe between 1939 and 1942, any economic problems in Germany would solve themselves. The territories, peoples and possessions that fell into her hands would surely provide enormous resources in food, capital and human labour. Yet these obvious gains did not bring the benefits that might have been expected. Two points help to explain this.

One is that while Hitler appeared to have mobilized the nation for a great war effort in 1939, he did not follow it through fully. It is true that rationing was introduced and kept throughout the war, but as Table 6 shows it was only in the last 18 months of the war that the population began to suffer real shortages and hardship. In fact, bread supplies were maintained until the very last month. As times began to get hard for the Germans, a bitter riddle did the rounds. It drew on the reputation of Ghandi, the Indian nationalist leader who was famous for his hunger strikes. 'Question: What is the difference between India and Germany? Answer: In India one man starves for the people; in Germany the people starve for one man.'

Bread	Meat	Fats	
Sept 1939	no limit	550	310
1940	2,400	450	280
1941	2,300	400	269
1942	2,125	356	206
1943	2,475	437	215
1944	2,525	362	218
Feb 1945	2,225	156	156
Mar	2,225	148	190
April	900	137	75

table 6 weekly food rations in Germany for 1 adult (in grams)

It is true that by 1941, 50 per cent of the German workforce was employed in military production of some sort, but this gave a false impression of the actual effort put in. Aircraft production increased only marginally between 1939 and 1941 and the number of tanks in that time crept up from 3,500 to only 4,300. Of course, had the war been over by late 1941, as it might well have been had the Russians and British been knocked out, which they very nearly were, the question of Germany's domestic war effort would never have arisen. But with the Soviet Union and Britain still in the fight, joined from 1941 on by the USA, Germany's war, far from being over, was only just beginning. The Germans had missed their opportunity economically and militarily. It was as if, without intending to, the German nation had allowed the brilliance of its army's campaigns between 1939 and 1941 to lull it into complacency.

A second factor is that there was no ministry or body with overall responsibility for organizing the war effort. This encouraged rivalry between government departments and the armed services and made a concerted effort difficult. Himmler and Goering often trod on each other's toes when trying to draw the lines of authority between their rival ministerial empires. Communication between departments was seldom smooth which meant that decisions and instructions were not always clear. It is a further reminder that Nazi Germany was never the monolithic super-efficient state that its own propaganda suggested and popular imagination believed.

The wartime economy under Speer, 1942–5

It was to remedy the problem that the lack of central co-ordination had created that Hitler called in Albert Speer. As with Schacht earlier, Speer was given a very large measure of freedom by Hitler to develop policies as he saw fit. Hitler said of him, 'He is an artist and has a spirit akin to mine. He is a building-person like me, intelligent, modest, and not an obstinate military-head.' From 1942 until the end of the war, Speer, as Minister of Armaments and War Production, wielded immense power in the ordering of the German economy. He used it skilfully and effectively. Despite the mounting pressure from bombing raids as the Allies gained control of the skies over Germany, Speer actually doubled German armaments production overall. To quote one example: when he took over as Armaments Minister in 1942, German factories had turned out 4,500 tanks; by 1944, Speer had raised that figure to 17,300.

Speer's skill was in introducing techniques that made the industrial plants flexible so that they could produce a greater range of armaments than before, thus enabling them to meet particular demands. He also pared away much of the bureaucracy that had grown around industry. Managers and workers had a clearer understanding of what was expected of them and what they could do. Transport and freight movement were streamlined so bottlenecks were avoided and materials reached the plants on schedule. Had the *Luftwaffe* still been able to provide protective cover, there is no saying how long Germany might have been able to sustain its war effort. As it was, it is arguable that without Speer's inspired organization of armaments production, Germany might have lost the war two years earlier than she did.

How well industry responded under Speer's leadership can be seen in Table 7, which indicates that he managed to sustain high output right through to 1944, even though for most of that time Allied attacks on Germany were causing severe damage to factories and plants.

	1941	1942	1943	1944
Steel (millions of tons)	31.8	32.1	34.6	28.5
Coal (millions of tons)	248.3	264.2	268.9	249.0
Synthetic oil (millions of tons)	4.1	4.95	5.7	3.8
Synthetic rubber (thousands of tons)	69	98	117	104
Aluminium (thousands of tons)	233.6	263.9	250.0	245.3

table 7 German industrial output, 1941–4

A major disappointment for Speer, though he was not responsible for it, was the failure of the autobahn, one of Hitler's great prestige projects, to aid the war effort. By 1941 over 3,000 km (2,000 miles) of motorway had been constructed. However, impressive though the 'Adolf Hitler highways' were as a piece of civil engineering, they made little sense economically. There simply was not enough motor traffic at the time to justify the great expense of building them. Nor did they prove of any great worth militarily. If Hitler had aimed to use them for strategic purposes he was to be disappointed. While troop transporters and light artillery could be moved along them, tanks could not; they were simply too heavy and dug into the concrete surface making the roadway unusable.

Despite the reputation that he later gained for having been one of the more morally scrupulous of the Nazi leaders, Speer was not above using slave labour in the interests of the Third Reich. By 1944, a quarter of Germany's workforce of 40 million was composed of foreigners. Some of these were voluntary workers from the nations allied with Germany, but the vast majority were forced labourers, deported to Germany and made to work in appalling conditions. Under the pressure of war, Speer paid scant attention to their suffering. Circumstances required that he regard them not as people but as economic units.

It was for this war crime that Speer was sentenced at Nuremberg to a 20-year prison term. He accepted his guilt and admitted that he had used slave labour and liaised with the SS in moving concentration camp prisoners into forced labour factories. But it was said in mitigation at his trial that 'in the closing stages of the war he was one of the few men who had the courage to tell

Hitler that the war was lost and to take steps to prevent the senseless destruction of production facilities.' That had indeed been the case. When the war had become a hopeless cause for Germany, Speer had rejected Hitler's 'annihilation rather than surrender' demand, refusing to carry out the senseless destruction orders he was given.

In striking ways, the fate of the economy parallels that of Nazi Germany itself. It began with high hopes, appeared to have established itself strongly and was then destroyed in an avoidable war.

08 the German armed forces, 1933–45

This chapter will cover:

- the structure of the armed forces
- the *Abwehr*
- the *Luftwaffe*
- the army
- the navy
- the power struggle between the Nazi Party and the army.

The armed services under Hitler

The overall title of the armed forces was the *Wehrmacht*, comprising the army, navy and air force. However, the term *Wehrmacht* was often used to refer specifically to the army. Figure 10 shows the overall shape of the command structure of the armed services.

Supreme Commander
Hitler

Air force	**Army**	**Navy**
Goering	Brauchitsch	Raeder

figure 10 command structure of the Wehrmacht, 1941

One of the most remarkable features of the *Wehrmacht* is the speed at which it grew under Hitler. In the 1919 peace settlement the Allies had forbidden Germany to have an army larger than 100,000. Hitler ignored that rule and by 1939 his rearmament drive had produced a *Wehrmacht* of nearly four and a half million men. During the six years of war that followed that number more than doubled:

	Army	Navy	Air force	Total
1939	3,740,000	122,000	677,000	4,539,000
1940	4,370,000	190,000	1,100,000	5,660,000
1941	5,200,000	404,000	1,545,000	7,149,000
1942	5,750,000	570,000	1,900,000	8,220,000
1943	6,550,000	780,000	1,700,000	9,030,000
1944	6,510,000	810,000	1,500,000	8,882,000
1945	5,300,000	700,000	1,000,000	7,000,000

table 8 strength of the armed services (in millions to the nearest 100,000)

To this figure should be added, the *Waffen SS* which was reckoned as a branch of the fighting forces. By the end of the war it numbered over three quarters of a million men.

Hitler and the army

Given German history with its strong military tradition and Hitler's notion that 1918 had not been a military defeat but a political betrayal, it was to be expected that he would lay stress on the role of the armed forces in the creation of the Third Reich.

The army officers tended to be conservative and suspicious of politics and politicians. One of Hitler's master strokes soon after coming to power was to make the army feel that it had a special relationship to him as leader of the nation. He did this by making the army take an oath of allegiance to him personally. The army welcomed this because, although it tied itself to Hitler, it also made itself independent of the Nazi Party and the State. General Werner von Blomberg pledged the army to Hitler's service in these words: 'The *Wehrmacht*, as the sole armed force of the entire nation, while remaining apart from the conflicts of internal politics, will express its gratitude by its devotion and fidelity.'

The military oath

I swear by God this holy oath, that I will render to Adolf Hitler, Leader of the German nation and people, Supreme Commander of the Armed Forces, unconditional obedience, and I am ready as a brave soldier to risk my life at any time for this oath.

Hitler's title, Supreme Commander, was not a courtesy title; it described the literal truth. He was the active commander of Germany's armed forces. Hitler was unique among the leaders of all the wartime nations in that he took the actual military decisions. When things went well from 1939 to 1942, he gained immense prestige in Germany as the great conquering warlord, which consolidated his already absolute position and made it difficult to oppose him effectively. Even when his generals doubted his judgement, they seldom spoke out or did so in such a hesitant manner that they were easily brushed aside.

This put him beyond open criticism and meant that any effective move against him by the army generals would necessarily be illegal and in breach of their oath of loyalty to him. The result was that critics within the army turned to conspiracy against Hitler rather than direct challenge to him. Nevertheless, those who conspired were always a very small minority. Many might complain about him in closed conversation, particularly after the tide of victories turned against Germany after 1942, but few were willing to go so far as to plan his removal, and fewer still to plot his death.

All this is a reflection of how divided the army was and why it was relatively easily outmanoeuvred by the political forces around Hitler. The generals' special relationship with Hitler, created in 1934 when they assisted him in breaking the SA, did not guarantee they would always get their way. Hitler's method of governing has been described as 'divide and conquer'. He seemed deliberately to leave the structure of authority under him unclear, so that no one individual or group had too much power.

He seemed not to mind that tensions and rivalry developed between the political and military powers because of this. In fact, he probably welcomed it. Since he was the absolute authority in both political and military affairs, he could afford to play off one group against another. Where he felt that his authority was coming under challenge, as with the SA, he could always call on force to crush it.

The army loses its independence

The army's loyalty to Hitler in the SA crisis in 1934 and its adoption of the special oath of personal allegiance to him had made the army independent of the Nazi Party. But independence is not the same thing as superiority. The balance between the military and political forces had still to be decided. Over the next four years relations between them were relatively smooth, but in 1938 another crisis intervened. It involved Werner von Blomberg, the general who in 1934 had persuaded the army of the benefits of the *Führer* oath.

Blomberg's reward had come in 1935 when he had been made Commander-in-Chief of the *Wehrmacht*, followed a year later by his elevation to the rank of Field Marshal, the first time Hitler had granted such a title. Blomberg's star was in the ascendant. But tragedy awaited. His chief political enemies, Goering and Himmler, jealous of his rise, were out to get him, Goering because he wanted Blomberg's job and Himmler because he wanted to assert the SS's authority over the army's.

Together, Goering and Himmler leaked information to Hitler about the Field Marshal's dubious private life. Blomberg had married twice, the second time unwisely. His second wife had a past; she had been a prostitute, specializing in obscene photographs of herself, some of which were still in circulation. Hitler was fed these details by Himmler and Goering, who had both acted as witnesses at Blomberg's recent wedding. The outcome was that Hitler asked for Blomberg's resignation and ordered him and his wife to leave Germany for a time. It was interesting how puritanical the Nazis could be when it served a political purpose.

Blomberg was not the only victim. A week after his fall from grace, his close colleague, Werner von Fritsch, Commander-in-Chief of the German Army was brought down by another scandal. Again, it was concocted by Goering and Himmler, who bribed a male prostitute to declare at a special meeting in Hitler's presence that Fritsch was a practising homosexual. Despite his desperate denials, Fritsch was not believed. A week later, Hitler formally announced that both Blomberg and Fritsch had resigned 'for health reasons'. Hitler then took the title of Commander-in-Chief for himself.

The lesson of the whole affair was that the days of an independent German army were over. It was no longer possible for generals to pretend that they could remain aloof from the politics of the nation. Goering and Himmler had reasserted the claims of the Nazi Party, Hitler's formidable control had been enhanced, and a further step had been taken in the politicizing of every major aspect of life in Nazi Germany.

The episode also suggested that the army leaders, as represented by Blomberg and Fritsch, were not impressive. Behind his back, Blomberg was mockingly called 'the rubber lion', denoting that though he occasionally snarled he was always willing to bend. They lacked strength of will and made poor political judgements. It might be objected that this is to judge them unfairly since, after all, they were not politicians but soldiers. But they were operating in a very political world. The Third Reich was a new society and in many respects under Hitler it made up its rules as it went along.

Blomberg never fully recovered from the experience and died a mumbling old man in American custody in March 1945. Fritsch lost his life in 1939 while serving as an active soldier in the Polish campaign. Those who saw it said it was almost as if he wanted to die. He walked deliberately towards a machine gun nest and was cut down in a hail of bullets.

The structure of the army

It is easier to draw lines on a chart than to describe the exact relation between individuals, groups and departments, but an idea of the army's command structure can be gained from Figure 11 showing the position in 1941.

How what is shown here worked in practice would depend on the character and abilities of the individuals and groups involved, but above all else the German Army had inherited a strong sense of discipline and obedience to orders. This meant it was a very effective force once in action. But its strong discipline by no means stifled initiative in the field. Indeed, officers lower down in the chain of command were encouraged to think tactically and adjust to the changing character of a battle or engagement.

This was not an invitation to ignore broad strategy, but was meant to make units quick and flexible in reaction. One of the habits inculcated into soldiers while training was for them 'to think two ranks ahead', that is to assume that the officers immediately above them had been removed, leaving them to work out how to respond now that orders were no longer coming down the line.

The German High Command (OKH) divided its forces into six main army groups which were each subdivided on a regional basis into divisions. Table 9 shows the main divisions as they were in 1939 and 1945.

	1939	1945
Panzers (armoured tanks)	6	31
Motorized	8	13
Infantry	88	177
Mountain	3	10
Total	105	231

table 9 army strength in divisions

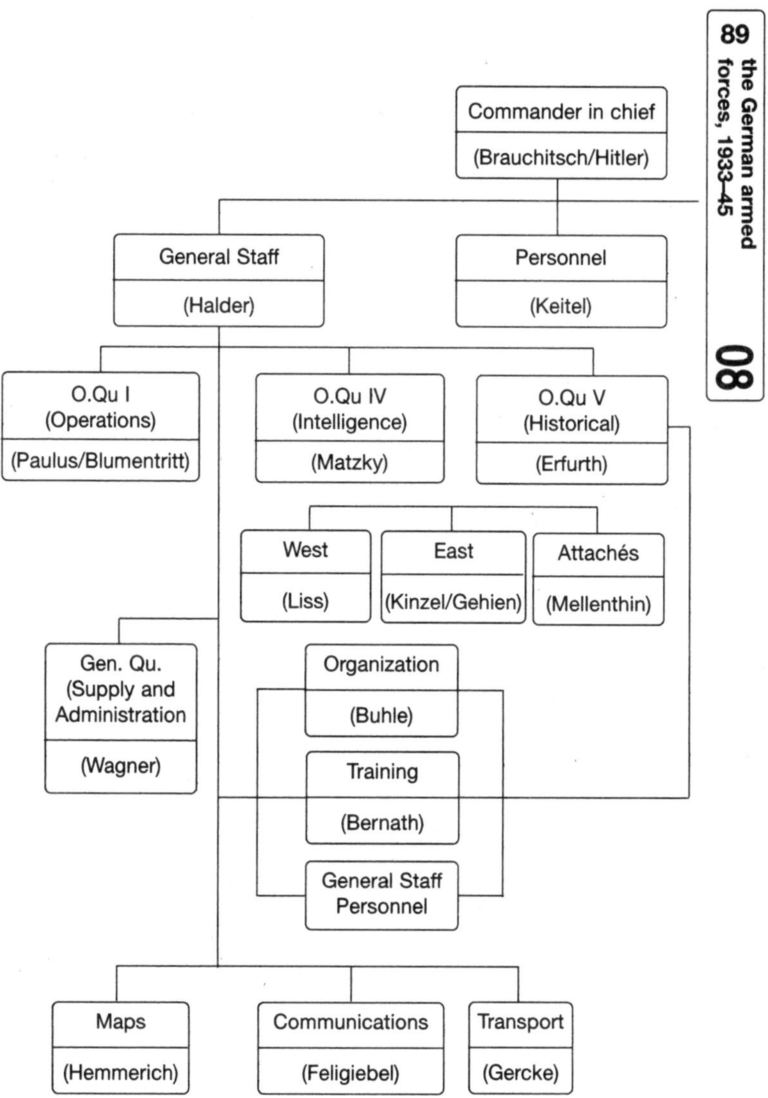

figure 11 chart showing the structure of the German High Command, 1941–2

The *Luftwaffe* (air force)

The *Luftwaffe* was unique among the German armed services. The army and the navy were built on existing systems whereas the *Luftwaffe* was wholly constructed within the Nazi period. The Versailles settlement had denied Germany the right to develop a military air force. When the *Luftwaffe* came into being, therefore, it was another act of Nazi defiance. Hitler placed great faith in aerial warfare. He believed it would be the deciding factor in any major conflict of the future. Consequently it was vital to develop a powerful *Luftwaffe*. Goering, an air ace of the Great War, was the obvious choice to be in charge.

However, Goering as head of the *Luftwaffe* did not have a good war. There was too much of the flamboyant showman about him rather than the consistent planner. He loved chatting to young pilots about their exploits and was readier to listen to their optimistic reports than to take heed of the dull but revealing figures prepared by his staff officers.

Despite being a very young service, the *Luftwaffe* quickly became a confused one. This was because Goering did not give a firm lead. He was both *Luftwaffe* chief and Minister of Aviation and often failed to make a clear distinction between the functions of the two posts. The *Luftwaffe* should have been concerned with operational matters, the Aviation Ministry with the provision of pilots, planes and hardware. But Goering often gave his officials instructions that did not come within their remit. This arbitrary crossing of administrative boundaries left the officials uncertain. Acute personal rivalries within departments did little to improve matters.

Although impressive figures were achieved in the building of aircraft, too little attention was given to the development of new types of plane. Some experts had argued for a long time that if the *Luftwaffe* was to meet the demands of a long war it needed strategic long-range bombers of the type used by the RAF and USAF. But the *Luftwaffe*'s preparations were geared to the short campaigns in which it had been so successful between 1939 and 1941. It was not ready for the type of war that developed after 1941.

On the positive side, Goering's engaging style did much to help morale and some of his pet ideas did prove important. One in particular was his creation of *Luftwaffe* parachute units which proved highly effective, for example, in the invasion of Crete.

The year 1940 ought to have been Goering's greatest moment as head of the *Luftwaffe*. Poland had been broken by *Blitzkrieg* the previous year. Now was the opportunity to defeat Britain solely from the skies. He had assured Hitler this could be done, but having allowed the BEF to escape from Dunkirk, he then lost the Battle of Britain by switching the *Luftwaffe* away from attacks on the fighter stations to night-time raids on the cities. The move saved Britain whose air defences were on the point of collapse.

The *Luftwaffe* proved no more successful on the Eastern Front. But its greatest failure was still to come. By 1943, the Allied bombing raids on Germany became unstoppable. Goering's once great air force was incapable of defending Germany. By the autumn of 1944, the *Luftwaffe* could hardly be said to exist.

The scale of the tragedy is evident in one particular set of figures. In the five months between January and May 1944, 2,262 pilots were killed in combat. Since the average number of pilots available each month was 2,283 this marked a *Luftwaffe* loss of 99 per cent of its operational pilots in that period. It was a tragedy from which the *Luftwaffe*, and indeed Germany, never recovered. It left the skies open to Allied bombing raids which, more than any other factor, accounted for Germany's defeat in May 1945.

Devastating though these losses were, fresh new pilots were trained and replacement planes were built, but what could not be produced was the fuel to power them. The *Luftwaffe*'s greatest need was fuel, and it was the lack of it that eventually made it impossible for it to remain in the skies.

The *Abwehr* (army intelligence)

The *Abwehr* (which best translates as 'for defence') was the Third Reich's secret service system which it inherited from Weimar. Up until 1933 it had been concerned exclusively with the prevention of spying, but after the Nazis came to power, the *Abwehr* began developing spy networks of its own. Initially, this was difficult since, under the Versailles Treaty, Germany was forbidden to engage in foreign espionage. But, as with so many other clauses of the Treaty, Hitler chose to ignore the prohibition. He appointed Wilhelm Canaris as *Abwehr* Chief, a navy captain with espionage experience going back to the Great War.

Canaris, who was a fluent linguist, quickly established spy cells in Spain and France, which brought in valuable information on foreign warships in the Atlantic and Mediterranean. He was less successful in his efforts to do the same in Britain and the USA; when the war started in Western Europe in 1939, Germany had still not created a reliable spy base in Britain.

An undoubted success in that year, however, was the *Abwehr*'s work in preparing the way for the successful invasion of Czechoslovakia. As it grew, the *Abwehr*, which added *Ausland* ('foreign lands') to its title to signify its more ambitious aims, included direct military action. Special *Abwehr* sabotage units operated behind enemy lines during the campaigns against Poland and the Soviet Union.

One of the problems for the *Abwehr* in Germany was that although it was technically an army organization it strayed frequently into non-military affairs. For example, it compiled dossiers on possible opponents of the Nazi regime. This brought it into dispute with the SD and the SS, which regarded civilian surveillance as their concern. This took a personal turn with the rivalry between Canaris and Heydrich, whose edgy relationship went back to the days when Heydrich had been a naval cadet under Canaris. Each threatened to reveal ruinous secrets about the other; namely, Heydrich's suspected Jewishness and Canaris's homosexuality.

In the end neither of them went through with their threats, but it was a further example of the personal tensions that often lay beneath the surface of the Third Reich.

Whatever credit the *Abwehr* had earned before and during the war was sullied in Nazi eyes when police investigations into its financial records revealed that some of its members had been lining their pockets through shady currency exchange deals with foreign bankers. The investigation followed accusations from the SD which was always looking to undermine its rival organization.

But there were even more serious matters. The *Abwehr* was suspected of becoming the centre of the resistance to Hitler. Since late 1941, Canaris, had believed that the expanded war into which Hitler had pushed Germany could not be won. He remained very uncertain about how far to let his doubts over Hitler go, but eventually he joined the plotters. This was after Hitler had dismissed him from his *Abwehr* post early in 1944 and given his intelligence responsibilities to Himmler. Arrested soon after the July Bomb Plot had failed, Canaris was held in Flossenberg concentration camp before being executed in April 1945.

The *Abwehr*'s disgrace extended beyond Canaris. In the later stages of the war, *Abwehr* agents used their spy network to make contact with the Allies with a view to negotiating a ceasefire and a compromise peace which would indemnify them against prosecution for war crimes. The *Abwehr* that had begun as a movement to counter subversion ended as a subversive movement itself.

The navy

German naval rebuilding in the Third Reich began with a major diplomatic development. In 1935, Germany signed a naval agreement with Britain which permitted her to develop a surface fleet of up to 35 per cent the size of Britain's, and a U-boat force of up to 45 per cent the size of Britain's. British reasoning was that if Germany was allowed to redevelop her navy she would be far less likely to be embittered and internationally dangerous. Moreover, the specific proportions that had been laid down in the agreement made it far easier to monitor the growth of the German navy. Britain could still feel she was monarch of the seas.

For Hitler, however, the agreement was a sign that the British no longer regarded the Versailles Treaty as binding. It added to his confidence that other breaches of the Treaty could be attempted with little protest from Britain.

With Germany free now to embark on a naval programme, the big question was what form should it take. Hitler did not believe that the actual figures agreed by Germany and Britain meant very much in practice. The principle of Germany's naval expansion had been conceded. Germany could build as it wished. This produced two simple but opposed schools of thought. One, favoured by the navy's overall commander, Admiral Raeder, was that priority should be given to the construction of a fleet of modern battleships.

The opposite view was that should a war come, the most likely opponent would be Britain. In naval terms, the best way to defeat her would be by crippling her merchant shipping, the strategy that had nearly won the war for Germany in 1917.

Therefore, the torpedo-firing U-boat was the vessel to develop. This was the argument strongly backed by Admiral Dönitz, a veteran of the submarine campaigns of the Great War.

The argument over priorities resulted in little naval construction being started in the 1930s. Eventually, in 1939, the navy strategists came up with Plan Z, approved by Hitler, which basically followed Raeder's proposal for a large surface fleet to be built. The year 1944 was quoted as the earliest time for the plan's completion. However, before anything could be done the war intervened and the plan was scrapped. The navy for the moment would have to fight with what it had.

Germany's naval strength, 1939

2 battleships, 3 pocket battleships, 6 light cruisers, 1 heavy cruiser, 21 destroyers, 12 torpedo boats, 57 U-boats

The way the war developed largely vindicated Dönitz's views. It was her submarines that gave Germany her greatest chance of success. Recognizing this, the navy put prodigious efforts into building new U-boats. The results are shown in Table 10.

1939	1940	1941	1942	1943	1944	1945
15	40	196	244	270	189	0

table 10 numbers of German U-boats built in wartime

Her surface warships did not have the strategic impact hoped for and the losses sustained, particularly the sinking in May 1941 of the great battleship *Bismarck*, which was scuttled after it had been left helpless in the water following the wrecking of its steering gear by a torpedo, were hard for the Germans to take.

Germany compensated by sustained 'wolf pack' U-boat attacks on Allied convoys that proved so successful that in 1942 the ratio of ships to submarines lost was 14:1. But from 1942 things took on a grimmer aspect for Germany as combined American and British convoys, greatly aided by the accurate intelligence reports that came from the breaking of the German Ultra code, began to cause heavy losses to the U-boats.

Allied Merchant shipping Losses (100,000 tons)

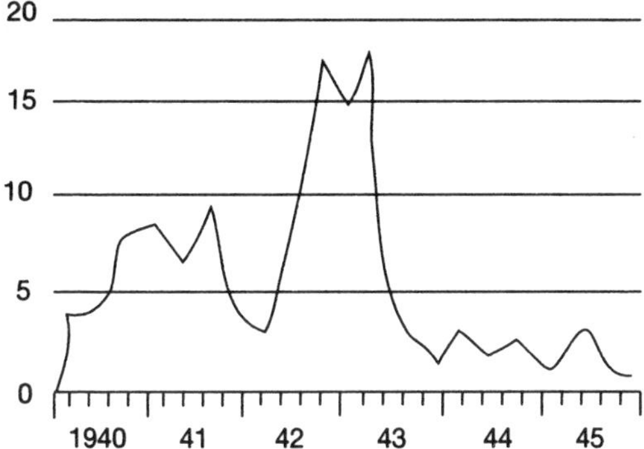

Number of operational U-boats

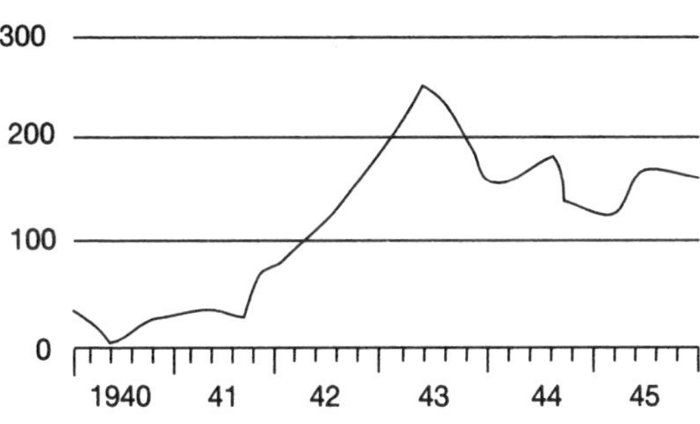

U-boat losses

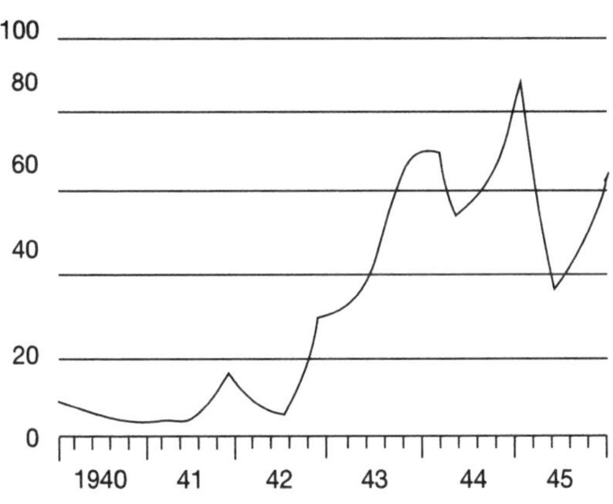

figure 12 graphs showing U-boat successes and losses, 1939–45

The navy sustained itself as a fighting force longer and more effectively than the army or the *Luftwaffe*, but it, too, in the end succumbed to the overwhelming weight of Allied arms ranged against it. How high a price Germany's armed forces paid stands out in Table 11:

Cause of death	Army	Navy	Air force	Total
Killed in action	1,622,561	48,904	138,596	1,810,061
Other causes	160,237	11,125	19,976	191,338
Missing (presumed dead)	1,646,316	100,256	156,132	1,902,704
Wounded	4,145,863	25,259	216,579	4,387,701

table 11 wartime losses in the German armed services, September 1939 to January 1945

To these figures should be added a further half a million deaths estimated to have occurred in the last three months of the war, February to May 1945.

This chapter will cover:

- the Nazi use of propaganda
- how the arts fared under Nazism
- how conditions changed for the workers
- Nazi treatment of undesirables.

Propaganda and the arts

As soon as Hitler was in power, Joseph Goebbels began to use the art of propaganda to inculcate the idea of the German nation unifying under the direction of the Nazi Party and its inspired leader, Adolf Hitler. A spectacular aspect of this were the great rallies often held at night by torchlight. Nuremberg was the major centre for these.

The talented film maker, Leni Riefenstahl (1902–2003), brilliantly captured the essence of these displays in her documentary, *The Triumph of the Will*, made in 1935. Her skilful use of camera angles, light and shade, close-ups, and sweeping panoramas portrayed Hitler as the man of destiny creating a Third Reich that expressed the will of the mighty German people. Nazi propaganda under Goebbels was a giant public relations exercise.

Goebbels let it be known that his aim was nothing less than the reformation of German culture. His Propaganda Ministry set themselves these essential tasks:

- to promote the German nation as the supreme form of social and cultural organiszation
- to rid the nation of all Jewish influences
- to develop the *Führer* principle – the notion of Hitler as the faultless leader to whom all Germans owed obedience
- to encourage pride in the Aryan race as the highest form of human development
- to develop German-Aryan arts free from the corruption of Jewish influences

In laying such stress on destroying Jewish influences, Goebbels was defining culture by what it was against, not what is was for. This was not a recipe for genuine cultural growth. Nazism was an attempt to impose what would now be called political correctness, trying to bully people into thinking along prescribed lines. It was really the opposite of creativity.

And this was how it proved. The arts did not flourish; they became dull and predictable. Since any hint of modernism was to be avoided, artists played safe, producing works that would not fall foul of Nazi censorship. Painting and sculpture glorified the myths of the German past and emphasized manly, heroic deeds. Abstract works were unacceptable. Art had to be formal and figurative. Some works, such as nude studies, were technically accomplished, but since they were painted or sculpted according to concepts of Aryan manliness and female virtue there was a coldness and predictability about them.

The arts seldom flourish under authoritarian regimes. Works produced in line with political correctness struggle to be creative. Music, perhaps the most abstract of the arts and, therefore, the most difficult to censor, fared better. Unless they were Jewish, composers tended to escape interference. However, directors of opera or ballet had to be careful that the storyline did not offend Nazi values.

Musicians, artists and thinkers

Many in the arts, however, did co-operate with the Nazi regime. The celebrated conductors Wilhelm Furtwängler and Herbert Von Karajan, and the renowned composer, Richard Strauss, were examples. It was Strauss who conducted at the opening and closing ceremonies of the Berlin Olympics and who composed new music for the occasion.

The argument was later put forward by Furtwängler that, since music transcended politics, he felt no guilt. But if he truly believed that, then why had he not protested against the ban on Jewish works such as those by Mahler, Schoenberg, Mendelssohn, and Hindemith? The fact was that so many German writers and artists, without being avid supporters of Hitler's Reich, were quite prepared to make the necessary artistic compromises in order to continue working under the Nazis.

However, some two and a half thousand artists and scientists went into voluntary exile rather than put up with political control. If they were Jewish, of course, their motive was not simply artistic freedom but sheer survival.

The philosopher, Martin Heidegger, represented the betrayal of which so many intellectuals were guilty when he called upon his colleagues and students to reject such notions as freedom of speech as corruptions and instead place themselves with entire obedience in the service of the new German Reich. There was a powerful religious impulse to Nazism. Hitler was the new Messiah. A Berlin professor declared that 'tomorrow has become today – the end of the world mood has been transformed to an awakening. The leader, yearned for and prophesied, has appeared.'

Radio

At a more down-to-earth level, Goebbels showed foresight in grasping the potential of radio as a way of communication. By 1933 he had established a Reich Radio Company (RRC), the sole purpose of which was to spread Nazi propaganda. He ordered the dismissal of any staff member not committed to the German cause and allowed no broadcast of any opinion critical of the regime. Quite shamelessly he told the RRC 'you are the creators of public opinion'. A vital development was a campaign to provide as many Germans as possible with radio sets. Between 1932 and 1937 the number of Germans with access to broadcasting rose from 22 to 70 per cent of the population.

Hitler and the arts

Hitler, like the Emperor Nero, saw himself as a great patron of the arts. He personally intervened to make sure that large subsidies went to the celebrated Bayreuth Festival which specialized in the operas of Wagner, his favourite composer. He once claimed to have attended seven consecutive performances of Tristan and Isolde, which is a sign of endurance if not good taste. A fascinating detail is that in the later stages of the war Hitler could not bear to listen to Wagner. As Berlin collapsed around him he preferred the escapist route and gave himself over to the operettas of Johann Strauss and Franz Lehar.

An interesting statistic is that despite the glorification of war in Nazi Germany some 20,000 artists and museum curators were exempted from national military service on the grounds that their cultural contribution to society was vital. An even more extraordinary aspect of this was that several hundred of those excused had Jewish blood.

On Hitler's instructions, museums, galleries, concert halls and opera houses were built in cities and provincial towns – with few questions asked about the cost. The biggest of all the galleries was built in his home town of Linz. It was here that he hoped to display the looted treasures brought back from the occupied territories, a project that was never realized after the war turned against Germany in the East.

Yet it is hard to think of Hitler as being genuinely cultured. He read little and his tours of galleries and exhibitions were official business, rather than personal pleasure. Even in art, the area where he supposedly had some knowledge, his tastes were limited and unimaginative. He liked formal figurative painting and sculpture but had no time for abstract works which he regarded as decadently Jewish.

The Berlin Olympics, 1936

Sport offered a great opportunity for propaganda. The Olympic Games proved a huge success. Goebbels and Goering excelled themselves in mounting magnificent displays of German organization and efficiency. The specially built athletics stadium held 110,000 spectators and was filled every day of the Games. Hitler also attended daily; his appearances occasioned massive outbursts of affection both in the stadium and along the crowd-thronged route. Berlin reverberated to the repeated cries of '*Sieg Heil*' ('hail to the victor'). At the dramatically staged opening ceremony, the Olympic hymn was preceded by the passionate singing by the crowd of the German national anthem and the Horst Wessel song.

Horst Wessel was an SA brownshirt thug who in 1930 had been shot dead by a tattooed pimp in a row over a prostitute. Since the pimp was also a Communist, the killing had a political edge. Wessel was elevated to the status of a martyr for Nazism. What helped was that he happened to have penned a poem in praise of the movement, the words of which were set to the tune of an old marching song. The first line went 'Oh raise the flag and close the ranks up tight!' Goebbels did not think much of the words or the tune, but he quickly realized the song's propaganda value as a cheap, emotional tear-jerker and encouraged its adoption as the Nazi anthem to be sung at every gathering of the National-Socialists.

Some four million spectators attended the Games. The foreign athletes, visitors and journalists who came to Berlin were invariably deeply impressed by the organization. Hitler, shrewdly judging that the international press would be appalled by open displays of anti-Semitism, personally ordered that the Nazi campaign against the Jews be suspended while the Games were on. The vicious signs and slogans disappeared from the streets and no anti-Jewish references were made in the press and the cinema or on the radio.

Much was later made of Hitler's anger at the success of Jesse Owens, the black American sprinter who won four gold medals.

It was said that he left the stadium early in disgust to avoid shaking hands with Owens. In fact, since Hitler did not meet any of the medal winners, it was not a direct snub. However he did confide to von Schirach, leader of the Hitler Youth, that he thought it disgraceful the USA should have included so many black athletes in its team.

But these were minor irritations that did not detract from the great propaganda success of the Games. It was also a great sporting success for Germany, whose athletes won more medals than those from any other country. This helped considerably in gaining recruits for the Hitler Youth.

The Hitler Youth

This was an organization run by Baldur von Schirach with the aim of training young men in National Socialist values that would last them for life. But it was not all politics. The Hitler Youth laid great emphasis on physical fitness and the outdoor life. In those respects it could be enjoyed in the way that scouting was in other countries. Grasping that the conformity of the young is a powerful weapon when it can be harnessed, the Nazis deliberately set out to give young people a particular sense of belonging to the new society that National Socialism was building. In 1939 membership of the Hitler Youth was made compulsory.

The character of Nazi propaganda

In retrospect, one can see that this remarkable development in public relations in the Nazi years was not confined to Germany. The 1920s and 1930s saw an explosion of advertising aimed at persuading the masses to buy consumer products. Sigmund Freud, the Jewish psychoanalyst, whose works were banned by the Nazis and who went to live in the USA acted as advisor to a number of commercial companies on the best techniques for inducing Americans to buy consumer products.

What was different about the German form of propaganda was the aim and purpose that accompanied it. It was essentially a corrupting process designed to reduce the complexities of social, economic and political life to a set of crude but convincing formulae. Hitler and National Socialism were the only hope and salvation for the nation. Germany's greatest enemies within were the Jews and the Communists, who were bent on destroying the Fatherland. The greatest enemy without was international Jewry which, in league with world Bolshevism, was preparing to undermine and overthrow the German state.

Goebbels set out to fulfil Hitler's assertion in *Mein Kampf* 'the people will more easily fall victims to a great lie than a small one.' Goebbels worked from the premise that repetition is the key to convincing people: the repeated slogan or phrase, the recurring image. Hitler had said in *Mein Kampf* that the masses of the people were not very intelligent; this made them easy to persuade and influence. Every aspect of modern technology of the day was used: radio, film, gramophone records, display boards and posters. What appeared everywhere were Hitler's name and image and the swastika.

A noticeable feature was how little real humour there was in all this. The little there was was of a bitter, destructive, anti-Semitic kind. On a road leading into Berlin a road sign read, 'Slow down dangerous bend ahead – Jews accelerate.'

A spectacular and frightening expression of the new cultural tyranny came in May 1933 in Berlin's Opera Square where on a huge pyre over 20,000 books, deemed as corrupt by the Nazis, were burned by exulting students. Among the Jewish texts that were confined to the flames were works by Freud, Einstein and a writer, Heinrich Heine, who at the end of the 18th century had delivered this terrifying prophesy, 'the burning of books will be followed by the burning of people.'

The German Labour Front

In the world of work, the single largest organization that affected the German people was the German Labour Front. This was begun in 1933 under the direction of Robert Ley, an alcoholic tough guy who had derived great pleasure from beating up Jews and Communists in the street violence that had been so much part of the Nazi movement in the 1920s. Ley was one of those Nazis who never quite made it to the top ranks of the party but whose work had a major impact on the German people.

Despite his addictions, he was a person of verve and enthusiasm who threw himself into the job with great energy. His aim as Director of the Front was to regulate the German workforce along military lines. He expressed this purpose in his motto,

'Every worker must regard himself as a soldier of the economy.' His first step towards this was to destroy the trade unions. Under the pretext of giving them a greater role in the economic life of the nation he made them part of the Front. This meant effectively that they came under state control and lost their independence. No longer were they entitled to take strike action or withdraw their labour. Wage rates and conditions were not negotiable; they were dictated by Ley from the top.

During the 12 years of the Third Reich, the Labour Front came to control 25 million workers. A very large bureaucracy and a very large budget were needed to organize such numbers. This provided plenty of opportunities for officials to make money for themselves by putting their hand in the till. Ley himself made a fortune by directing funds into his own pocket.

This did not stop him from presenting the Labour Front as the summit of Nazi ideals. Although described by a colleague as being 'intellectually a nonentity', Ley was given to flights of fancy. He spoke of ending all class conflict in Germany by creating 'social peace'. Workers and people would come together in the *Volk*, a word much used by Hitler to denote the sense of unity felt by a nation composed of the racially pure. They would work together for the good of Germany, willingly subordinating themselves as individuals to the collective will of the nation. To heighten the sense of solidarity workers were encouraged to wear identical blue uniforms.

What all this stuff and nonsense meant in plain terms was that German workers had to do what they were told. It was the Front's officials who decided who could be employed and where, who was to be promoted or dismissed, and what they were to be paid. This control increased after Germany went to war.

Yet it would be wrong to regard the Labour Front simply as a mechanism of oppression. Its military-style discipline did not rule out a strong commitment to workers' welfare. Insurance schemes that paid sickness, injury and bereavement benefits to deserving workers were put in place. Schooling was provided for the workers' children, and adult education was available to the workers themselves.

Recreational needs were catered for by the Labour Front's sponsoring of one of the most remarkable social experiments in Nazi Germany, the *Kraft durch Freude* (KDF – 'strength through joy') movement. The KDF was organized leisure for the masses. It covered everything: theatre, concerts, opera, musicals, lectures, dancing, and sports of every kind. Ley spoke of its offering 'the best of the best in food for the soul, the mind, and body.'

An especially successful scheme was the provision of holidays for the workers and their families. Special hotels and campsites, invariably of a very high order of comfort, were set up; one consequence was a great boom in the 1930s in tourism within Germany. In all, some ten million Germans, over one in seven of the population, were involved in KDF activities at some point between 1933 and 1943.

In purely material terms, leaving aside questions of enforced conformity, there is no doubt that, up until 1942, German workers had never had it so good. After that, however, things were to change.

To sustain her massive war effort, Germany needed a huge labour force. To meet this demand, Fritz Sauckel, Hitler's Minister of Labour, introduced a massive labour conscription programme in April 1942:

> Our armed forces of Greater Germany have surpassed themselves on the Eastern Front, in Africa, in the air and on the sea. To ensure their victory, it is now necessary to produce more and better weapons, equipment and ammunition through the increased efforts of the entire German people, the workers, the women and the whole of German youth.

The good days would soon be over. Behind Sauckel's words was the recognition that Germany had begun to overstretch herself. During the next three years the grimness of the wartime conditions in Germany with its very high civilian casualty rate destroyed the KDF as well as putting the Labour Front under increasing strain.

The euthanasia and sterilization programme

Behind the spectacular displays, the music and the marching, something very wrong was happening in Nazi Germany. It was killing its own people. Nazi ideas of racial purity required that undesirables – the mentally or physically disabled – were to be eliminated.

The demand that this be done intensified as war began to put pressure on food and resources. But it was not simply a reaction to war. The euthanasia programme was the logical development of Hitler's dismissal of the handicapped as 'useless eaters', who consumed vital supplies but could never give anything back to society.

An organization, code-named T4, was set up to oversee the identification and elimination of defectives and the sterilization of those weaker members of society who might pass on hereditary diseases. It required the co-operation of the medical profession to run the programme.

T4 set up seven killing centres at various places in Germany. Resembling hospitals or clinics, these were responsible for 70,000 deaths during the period of the Third Reich. At one of the centres, Hadamar, in southern Germany, officials organiszed a special celebration, during which toasts were drunk and congratulatory speeches made, to mark the killing of the 10,000th victim. At Hadamar, the technique employed was to group patients in a specially constructed air-tight chamber and then pump in carbon monoxide. All the bodies, except those kept back for dissection, were then carried on trolleys to the crematorium to be incinerated.

The method for murdering babies or young children was less dramatic; they were given lethal injections or simply left to die of thirst in rooms where their whimperings could not be heard.

The mental asylums were the obvious places to begin the programme. The usual method was to tell the selected patients that they were being taken in buses from the asylum for special treatment. Since those selected never returned, it soon became whispered knowledge among the inmates that to be selected was to be marked for death.

On occasion, this led to scenes of panic and resistance when the buses arrived. Force had to be used to restrain the desperate victims and force them aboard. Some accepted their fate with resignation. There were also examples of extraordinary dignity amidst the horror. On learning that she was on the list of those to be taken away, a young epileptic woman in a Stuttgart asylum wrote this wrenching letter to her father in October 1940:

> Dearest Father,
>
> Unfortunately, it cannot be otherwise. Today I must write these words of farewell as I leave this life for an eternal home. This will cause you much, much heartache. But I think I must die as a martyr. Father, good Father, I do not want to part from you without asking you and all my dear brothers and sisters once more for forgiveness for all that I have failed you in throughout my entire life. May the dear Lord God accept my illness and this sacrifice as a penance for this.
>
> Best of fathers, don't hold anything against your child, who loved you very profoundly; always think that I am going to heaven, where we will all be united together with God and our deceased dear ones. I won't lament, but shall be happy. I send you this little picture by way of a memento, your child will be meeting the saints in this way too.
>
> I embrace you with undying love and with the firm promise I made when we last said our goodbyes, and I will persevere with fortitude.
>
> Your child Helene
>
> On 2 October 1940. Please pray a lot for the peace of my soul. See you again, good father, in heaven.

Helene's father, who was a doctor, tried desperately to save her. He appealed for her exemption on the grounds that epilepsy was not on the list of incurable diseases that warranted 'special treatment'. But he was too late; he received a formal letter from the health authorities regretting his daughter's death, which had been the result of 'breathing problems'. This was literally true, of course. With her last breath she had sucked carbon monoxide into her lungs.

What the euphemisms and evasions used by the authorities indicated was that they well knew that if the true nature of their programme of death was made public it would be impossible to continue with it. The result was a conspiracy of silence among a large part of the medical profession. Death certificates were completed in such a way that they hid the real causes of death.

The T4 authorities issued doctors with a set of 60 suggested formulae from which to choose, according to the age and previous condition of the deceased.

> Pneumonia is an ideal cause of death because the population at large always regard it as a critical illness.
>
> Strokes. This cause of death is especially suitable in the case of older people; in the case of young people it is so rare that one should not use it.

Some doctors did protest by refusing to participate in the programme. A Dr Friedrich Hölzel turned down the post offered him of 'head of Children's Euthanasia' in Eglfing-Haar Asylum with these words: 'It is repugnant to me to carry this out as a systematic policy after cold-blooded deliberation and according to objective scientific principles, and without any feeling towards the patient.'

Others, without openly disobeying the authorities, found ways of saving some of their patients. One trick was to claim that listed inmates were so important as maintenance workers or assistants to the staff that the asylum could not afford to lose them. Most doctors and nurses, however, remained silent and participated in the programme. The chance of advancing their career or, more mundanely receiving extra food rations for themselves or their families, overcame their moral scruples.

There were many examples of relatives demanding that the deaths of members of their family be fully explained. The standard response from the authorities was initially to commiserate with the family and then use threats if they persisted with their questions. One father, who could not understand why his schizophrenic son could have been so healthy one day but suddenly die the next, pressed for a proper explanation. He was finally brow-beaten into silence by a menacing letter, part of which read:

> In the course of the year we repeatedly detect the ingratitude of relatives of *hereditarily ill* mental patients ... The nature and tone of your letter gives me cause to view you in a psychiatric light. I cannot refrain from notifying you that in the event you do not cease burdening us with letters, I will be compelled to have you examined by the public health doctor ... You are dealing with a public authority, which you cannot assail when you feel like it.

How seriously the authorities meant such threats to be taken was evident from an episode involving Gerhard Braune, a pastor of the Lutheran Church in Gallneukirchen. Braune, having heard rumours of a secret euthanasia programme being run at the local asylum, did some research which revealed that in the space of two months over 2,000 inmates had inexplicably died. Appalled, Braune wrote an open letter to Hitler himself, quoting this horrific figure. It is doubtful that the letter ever reached the *Führer*. What is certain is that within days of sending it, Braune was arrested and sent to prison for three months.

Strong-arm tactics were also used to silence the inhabitants of areas near the extermination centres who asked what was going on. The crematorium chimneys attached to one such centre at Hartheim gave off a thick, oily, black smoke which filled the air with strands of human hair and produced such a foul stench that locals vomited. When they gathered in the town to protest they were visited by one of the T4 administrators who told them that if they continued to complain they would be either shot or sent to a concentration camp.

The words from a sermon delivered by a pastor to his deaf congregation capture the distorted values of the time:

> You dear friends, you are afflicted with deafness. How burdensome it is! Certainly you must have asked yourself – why do I have to be deaf? And how unhappy your parents must have been when first they learned you could not hear. You must not transmit this affliction to your children and your grandchildren. You must remain childless. The authorities have ordered no one is to speak about sterilization, not even yourselves. Take note. You are to tell no one about it, not even your relatives. Trust in God. And do not forget the words of the Bible. You know that all things turn out for the best for those who love God.

There was a residual sense of decency which the Nazis realized they had to allow for. That is why, when news of the sterilization and euthanasia programme did leak out, there was unease and even some protests. A number of Protestant and Catholic clergy spoke out against it from the pulpit. In consequence, the programme was officially abandoned and the murder centres closed. But it was not the end of the story. The equipment used in the killing and the disposal of the bodies was not dismantled; it was simply sent to the death camps of the occupied East.

To take one area of disability, some 17,000 deaf people were sterilized. There was an appeals procedure that could be invoked, but of all those who appealed against sterilization only 5 per cent were successful. Health officials would visit schools and take away nominated children.

Since there was no national register of deaf people, the grim truth was that the details of children with disability were passed on to the authorities by their teachers and carers. It was they who informed on the children.

It is another of those disturbing pieces of evidence that illustrates that many of the policies of the Nazi regime could not have been carried out without the co-operation of ordinary Germans. One little boy, who had been the liveliest and naughtiest in his class, was taken away for 'treatment'. When he returned his classmates could not understand why he did not make jokes or play the fool anymore. They did not know he had been sterilized.

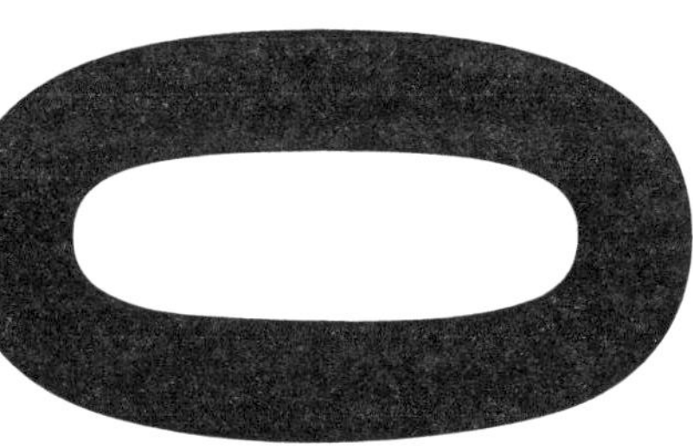

the instruments of Nazi control

This chapter will cover:

- the role of the SA
- the extent and power of the SS
- the character of the Gestapo
- how the Gestapo shaped German life.

The SS became the main system by which Nazi Germany throughout its 12 years of existence controlled the German people and enforced conformity on them. It gained its position by overthrowing the SA which had been the first Nazi organization concerned with protecting Hitler and the Party.

The SA

The SA (*Sturmabteilungen* or 'Storm troopers') were what might be described as Hitler's heavy mob. In the rough, tough world of Germany's streets in the 1920s, where extremist political groups battled with each other, it was essential to have physical protection. Quickly realizing this, Hitler set up the SA as his strong-arm guards. Recruited from the droves of rootless, unemployed or poorly employed young men who were to be found in most of Germany's cities in the 1920s, the SA was a haven for thugs.

But these were thugs who were given a sense of purpose. It must be remembered that not all of them were stupid, though many of them were. They were capable of responding to the arguments and appeals that Hitler put to them. Kitted out in their brownshirt uniforms, they felt a sense of brotherhood and belonging. The love of violence that is found in most young men who are not socially trained was cynically but cleverly exploited by the SA leaders.

Others simply joined on a whim. It was not a matter of profound thought being followed by a clear decision to join a particular party. In an atmosphere of violence, punching heads and bawling slogans is much more fun than thinking. The Communists, the Nazis main opponents, were not above being violent themselves.

They were just as prepared to beat up their rivals as their rivals were to beat up them. It is noticeable that around this time in Europe all the extremist political parties, whether left or right, used street violence to intimidate their rivals and impose themselves on society. Lenin's Russia, Mussolini's Italy, and Hitler's Germany all told the same story.

How easily people could change sides in this violent atmosphere and what a game it was to many of them was described by a young, Rhineland factory worker in 1933:

> Once it was all red flags, stars, hammers, sickles, pictures of Stalin and Workers of the World Unite! I used to punch the heads of anyone singing the Horst Wessel song. It was all the *Red Flag* and the *Internationale* then! You should have seen me! Street fights! We used to beat hell out of the Nazis, and they beat hell out of us. We laughed ourselves silly. Then suddenly when Hitler came to power, I understood it was all nonsense and lies. I realized Adolf Hitler was the man for me. My old pals? We're all in the SA now.

It was Ernst Röhm who built the SA into a highly effective instrument for advancing Nazism. Recruiting from the large numbers who had been made jobless by the depression, he increased its membership from 70,000 in 1930 to 170,000 a year later.

The intimidatory methods used by the brownshirts were highly successful in silencing opponents. Their marches, their singing and their torchlight processions advertised Nazism to the German people. They played a key role in the election campaigns between 1930 and 1933 that proved the stepping stones to Hitler gaining power.

Röhm was an old-style revolutionary. For him, the socialist part of National Socialism was what mattered; he wanted the workers and soldiers to run society, not self-seeking, privileged politicians. His misjudgement was to think that Hitler shared his belief in revolution. He thought that, like him, Hitler wanted the old German privileged society broken by force. He did not grasp that Hitler, having come to power by legal means, wished to consolidate the new Nazi state by winning over, not destroying, the traditional classes in Germany.

Soon after becoming Chancellor, Hitler declared that the revolution now had to stop and Germany had to consolidate before it could rebuild. It was something that Röhm never understood. He became impatient with his leader, remarking that Hitler was wooing the middle and conservative classes and forgetting where his original supporters had come from – the streets.

It was Hitler's growing awareness that the SA had come to represent a form of Nazism that he no longer wanted that convinced him it had to be removed. By the end of 1933, Hitler's first year in power, recruitment to the SA following the Nazi victory had swelled its ranks to over 4 million. For Hitler it was a worrying number. He could not afford to wait and risk the SA becoming an over-mighty force. Röhm spoke early in 1934 of the SA under him as 'a people's army', a concept that frightened the generals and businessmen whose support Hitler was anxious to gain. Without openly challenging Hitler, Röhm had clearly gone too far. No matter what Röhm's political intentions may have been, Hitler could no longer trust him. The SA would have to go.

Goering and Himmler hated Röhm; they wanted him out of the way and the SA subordinated to their organization, the SS. They added to Hitler's growing doubts about the SA leader, by telling him of the homosexual orgies in which the SA leader indulged in his spare time. It was tittle-tattle, but it helped convince Hitler that Röhm, the man who more than any other had helped bring him to power, was not worth saving.

In June 1934, in the episode known as the Night of the Long Knives, Röhm, along with other SA leaders, was arrested and shot. The SA was not immediately disbanded, but without its leaders it was impotent. It limped on, but its place had been usurped by more powerful bodies.

The SS

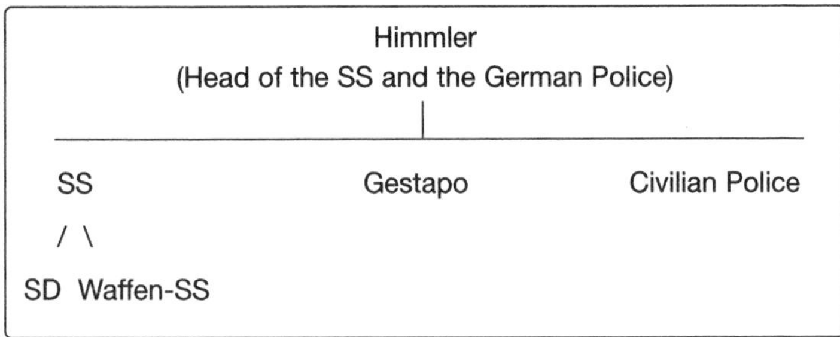

figure 13 Nazi instruments of state control

The SS (*Schutzstaffeln* – 'protective squads') began as Hitler's personal bodyguard in Munich in 1924. He encouraged the setting up of similar protective squads to guard Nazi officials in other cities. They mirrored, but at first did not challenge, Röhm's SA. In 1929, Heinrich Himmler took over the co-ordinating of these squads. He saw in them a means of developing a powerful control system within the Nazi Party and eventually within Germany itself, but for the moment he would have to wait until the SA had been disposed of. Himmler spent the time building up the SS with the result that on the eve of Hitler becoming Chancellor in January 1933 it had over 50,000 members, and by the end of that year some 200,000. This was still much smaller than the SA. But the SA's days were numbered. In June 1934 it was soon destroyed in the Night of the Long Knives, a dramatic move which Himmler helped plan.

With Röhm and the SA out of the way, the road was open for Himmler to advance the SS as an elite body, enforcing the law but ironically operating outside the law, since it was a party not a state organization. It was answerable only to Adolf Hitler. Although it later developed a military wing, the *Waffen-SS*, it was basically a civilian police network run on military lines.

One of the first tasks the SS undertook was the running of the concentration camps. Theodor Eicke was appointed national Inspector of the camps. Described by a fellow Nazi as a 'dangerous lunatic', Eicke had an interesting CV. He had earlier been dismissed from the SS but had been allowed back in after taking treatment at a psychiatric hospital. He had then become Commandant at Dachau before coming to Berlin in June 1934 to take part in the suppression of the SA. He had the distinction of being the guard who shot Röhm after the SA leader had refused to take his own life.

Eicke used his demented abilities to centralize the camp system and lay down a standardized pattern of brutality in accordance with his guiding principle, 'tolerance is weakness'. It was Eicke who created a special SS Death's Head Division to guard the camps. Its members, who were not fully trained soldiers but who knew enough about guns to be able to shoot prisoners, wore the skull and cross bones emblem on their caps.

By 1936, Himmler had succeeded in bringing the police forces of all the German states under the authority of the SS. These included the so-called 'political police', which dated back to the days of the Weimar Republic when the government had granted the local states the right to set up special investigation departments to track down extremist opponents of the Republic. They now provided a very convenient apparatus for extending Nazi control. The most notorious example of this was the Gestapo.

Himmler described the SS under him as 'the embodiment of the National Socialist idea'. His insistence on the elite nature of the SS meant that it guarded its membership very carefully. Entry to any posts within it involved the applicants being grilled about their background, their beliefs, and above all their race. From the first Himmler claimed that the SS must be built on 'the values of blood and selection'. Its great task was to maintain the racial purity of the German people. What this meant in practice was the persecution of the Jews. What bound the SS together, and indeed all the other institutions of the Third Reich, was anti-Semitism.

Himmler asserted that there were four fundamental principles that the SS must abide by themselves and seek to instil in the German people: protection of Germany from racial defilement; cultivation of a fighting spirit; loyalty to the German state; and absolute obedience of the orders of the *Führer*. For all Himmler's talk of protecting the people, it was the people he saw as the enemy. It was from them as much as from any external foe that a threat to the German nation could arise. In a talk to a group of *Wehrmacht* officers in 1937, he remarked:

> In a future war we shall not only have the Army's front on land, the Navy's front at sea and the Air Force's front in the skies over Germany, but we shall have a fourth theatre of war: the home front! There are the grass roots which we must keep healthy by hook or by crook because otherwise the three others, the fighting parts of Germany, would once more be stabbed in the back.

Whether he intended it or not, he had given in these words a perfect definition of the police state.

The SD

By 1939, the SS had added its own intelligence service to all its other organizations. The SD (*Sicherheitsdienst* – 'security service'), which had been started in 1934, was independent of the army's *Abwehr* but operated on similar principles. It engaged in a form of internal counter espionage with the aim of exposing enemies of the state and the party. Its actions sometimes overlapped with those of the Gestapo, but disputes between the two organizations tended to be settled quickly for fear of security being broken.

The Gestapo

The Gestapo (*Geheime Staatspolizei*, 'state secret police') grew out of the Prussian political police force to become one of the most fearsome features of Nazi Germany. Seizing on the powers of surveillance, arrest and interrogation which had originally been granted to the old police force during the Weimar Republic, the Gestapo developed into a nationwide organization. It took on the task of pursuing what it defined as 'enemies of the state'. This meant it could arrest and detain anyone on suspicion. The ordinary uniformed police force was subject to its authority. There was no legal restriction on its powers of arrest or its methods of interrogation. Torture became standard practice. Since it operated outside the ordinary court system, the Gestapo had no obligation to apply the normal rules of evidence. Suspects were assumed to be guilty. Concentration camps began to fill up with those arrested by the Gestapo.

The Gestapo's powers were also retrospective. That is, they could make crimes out of actions that had not been illegal when first performed. For example, those who had opposed Hitler before 1933 were regarded as suspect even though they might support him now that he was in power. Because of their past, they were still regarded as enemies to be hunted down. The following instruction from Berlin headquarters to a local branch in 1936 illustrates this:

> A list must be sent by return of post of those people in your area who were prominent in opposing and slandering the National Socialist movement before the take-over of power. The following details are required – the first name and surname, the date and place of birth, whether or not a Jew, present domicile, profession including all offices held by the person concerned. At the same time, a detailed report must be made about the incidents in which the individual was involved, particularly hostile activity towards the NSDAP.
>
> (22 April 1936)

Of all the terrors associated with Nazism, the Gestapo was arguably the most fearful for ordinary Germans. The very sound of the word Gestapo became frightening. It evoked the screech of car wheels just before dawn, the violent hammering on the door, the arrests in front of terrified wives and bewildered children, the screams of tortured 'enemies of the state' as they tried not to implicate themselves or betray their friends, and the roar of lorries as they drove off to deposit their despairing occupants at the gates of the camp.

Yet we need to be cautious here. The fact is that, for all its terror, the Gestapo depended on the support of the people at large. The organization simply was not big enough to have imposed itself without co-operation from the German public. One of the intriguing and disturbing facts that has come to light is that the Gestapo and the SS gained a great deal of their knowledge not from their own investigation but from information provided by ordinary citizens who were prepared to shop their neighbours and workmates. For example, in the town of Württemberg 70 per cent of arrests made by the Gestapo were on the basis of information given to the authorities by members of the public.

It was obviously not always a tale of tyrannous secret police imposing themselves on a cowed population; as often it was a story of people willingly betraying their associates.

The *Waffen-SS*

The *Waffen-SS* were the special military units that were created in 1939. Their origins went back as far as 1934 when a group of armed SS men known as the 'Political Readiness Squad' were involved in the arrest and killing of the SA leaders in the Night of the Long Knives episode. Hitler let it be known that, though such squads were technically illegal, he approved of them nonetheless. In the 1930s they carried out various raids on premises thought to contain 'enemies of the people' and hunted down political suspects. This was little different from the activities of the Gestapo and it was not until war came in 1939 that the essentially military character of these squads was recognized when they were renamed the *Waffen-SS*, which translates as 'SS strike force'.

Specially selected from SS volunteers, this force prided itself on being better trained and more dedicated than any of the other armed services. Entrants were carefully chosen for their bodily strength and physique and were meant to represent the Aryan ideal. The training was arduous and demanding. The aim was to produce toughness of body and mind. The character of this toughness, which was to exclude false sentiment based on traditional humanitarian values, was graphically expressed in a speech Himmler gave to SS officers in 1943:

> Our basic principle must be the absolute rule for the SS man; we must be honest, decent, loyal, and comradely to members of our own blood and to nobody else. What happens to a Russian or to a Czech does not interest me

> in the slightest. What the nations can offer in the way of good blood of our type we will take, if necessary by kidnapping their children. Whether other nations live in prosperity or perish through hunger interests me only in so far as we need them as slaves of our culture. Whether or not ten thousand Russian females drop down from exhaustion while digging an anti-tank ditch interests me only so far as the anti-tank ditch is completed for Germany.

In the face of strong opposition from the regular army, the SS before 1939 had limited its *Waffen* contingent to 23,000 men. But, with the coming of war, the numbers rapidly expanded. The *Waffen-SS* was able to put 38 divisions into the field, the first five formed being all panzer units. By 1945, over three-quarters of a million men had served in the *Waffen-SS*, a quarter of them being killed.

The *Waffen-SS* was not exclusively German. Soon after the start of the war, divisions were formed in allied or conquered countries. It is worth listing the non-German divisions: Albanian, Belgian, Belorussian, Croatian, Danish, Dutch, Estonian, French, Hungarian, Italian, Latvian, Norwegian, Romanian, Russian, Serb, Ukrainian. By the end of the war over half of the *Waffen-SS* was made up of recruits from outside Germany. As the casualties among German troops grew heavier, it became increasingly necessary to draw on other nationals. Some of the worst horrors of the war were committed by non-German *Waffen-SS* units, fighting on the side of the Third Reich.

While it was not technically part of the *Wehrmacht*, the *Waffen-SS* became a vital part of the armed forces after 1941. However, it was deeply disliked by the army generals who resented its political origins and its independence. What earned it its fearsome reputation was that, as a special force, it did not regard itself as bound by the accepted rules of warfare. It was guilty of some of the most appalling atrocities of the war.

Waffen-SS divisions fought on every front except North Africa. They played an increasingly significant role in the later campaigns of the war when the situation for Germany appeared hopeless. Fanatically committed to National Socialism, the *Waffen-SS* refused to accept surrender as an option. Their savage ruthlessness was mixed with extraordinary courage and an unremitting resolve to fight to the death. This was another frightening example of the misplaced idealism that Hitler and the Third Reich were capable of inspiring.

women in the Third Reich

This chapter will cover:

- Nazi attitudes towards women
- Hitler's view of women
- the role women played in the Third Reich
- the training and education of young women
- the difference that the war made to women in Germany.

Nazi attitudes towards women

It has often been said that before the 20th century the lives of German women were governed by the three Ks – *Kinder* ('children'), *Kirche* ('church'), and *Kuche* ('kitchen'). This may have been an oversimplification, but it was the case that women had not played a prominent role in political, social and economic life.

However, this appreciably changed in the first 30 years of the 20th century. The rapid growth of industry and the war effort of 1914–18 meant that many women went to work in factories and offices. The high number of German men killed in the war left a post-war gap. It is calculated that some 2 million women who might otherwise have married were forced by circumstance to remain single. Most of these took up jobs. An important result was that attitudes changed. German women became much more independent and began to think in terms being fully emancipated. The restrictive world of the three Ks was no longer acceptable.

This, however, did not fit in with Nazi thinking. From its foundation in the 1920s, the NSDASP had barred females from membership. Where women had appeared it was usually as shadowy background figures, noted for their relationship to men rather than being significant in their own right. Nazism was very much a male movement in tone and character. Its emphasis on physical struggle, toughness and military-style camaraderie, such as that shown by the SA, left no place for feminine values.

It would be difficult to think of anyone more old-fashioned in his views of women than Adolf Hitler. His plans for a new Germany certainly did not include the advancement of women. Specifically addressing women at a Nuremberg Party rally in 1934, he stated:

> If the man's world is said to be the State, his struggle, his readiness to devote his powers to the service of the community, then it may be said that the woman's is a smaller world. For her world is her husband, her children, her home. The two worlds are not antagonistic. They complement each other; they belong together just as man and woman belong together.

He simply did not accept women as equals. He defined female emancipation as a Jewish idea deliberately designed to weaken society. On another occasion he revealingly remarked:

> I detest women who dabble in politics. And if their dabbling extends to military matters, it becomes utterly unendurable. In no local section of the Party has a woman ever had the right to hold even the smallest post.
>
> (Hitler, January 1942)

Although some local Nazi women's organizations, such as the Leipzig Women's Group, were eventually permitted, they were looked on patronizingly and not allowed to join the main Party. In 1931, Gregor Strasser, an SA leader, acted on Hitler's order by closing down the separate women's groups and bringing them all into the NSF (National Socialist Womanhood). The purpose of the NSF was to keep Nazi women firmly under the control of the exclusively male Party.

One of Hitler's particular concerns was that the birth rate was dropping in Germany. This was partly a consequence of fewer marriages because of the lack of men, but it was also due to the availability of contraceptives; women were now able to limit their families. This trend disturbed Hitler; he wanted women to embrace motherhood as an ideal.

Nazi restrictions on women

Nazi policy after 1933 was in keeping with Hitler' views. Women were encouraged to give up work, return to the home and become mothers for the greater good of the nation. With the help of the NSF, which always claimed to be looking after the real needs of women, the government introduced measures to limit their prospects. Entry to university became more restricted, the professions provided fewer positions, and the civil service closed its doors. So that it was not all negative, women were offered special grants as an incentive to them to give up their jobs.

Motherhood campaigns

With these restriction on women in the work place went a major propaganda campaign to promote the concept of the ideal German woman. A favourite theme was to show her as a nursing mother whose milk gave life to the child and to the nation. Mother's Day in May 1934 was turned into a national celebration in which all the family were to share. Mothers who would normally have worked but who stayed at home on this Sunday were to be issued with a special 'Mother's Cross' medal.

Propaganda painting of the nursing mother. *Courtesy*: *akg-images*.

Fathers were given paid leave from work and school children were asked to paint pictures and write poems in praise of their mothers. How far all this was meant to go was clear from an order from Goebbels' Propaganda Ministry:

> In all the churches on this day the theme 'mother' and 'motherhood' must be addressed from the pulpit. The theatres can be put into service, both through the staging of appropriate and worthy plays and through the distribution of free tickets. These tickets must be for the whole family or single tickets for mothers whose children have already left home, especially for lonely old widows.
>
> (Goebbels, April 1934)

Nazi puritanism

Campaigns of this kind continued for most of the 1930s. Birth control clinics had to close and it was emphasized that abortion was an illegal act both for the woman concerned and the abortionist. There is a bitter irony in abortion being denied to German women at the same time as it was adopted as official policy as a way of getting rid of undesirables. But these were matters that went unnoticed or unremarked on by most Germans at the time.

In a mixture of puritanism and racism, the authorities strongly discouraged women, particularly if they were mothers, from wearing make-up. It was described as a Jewish habit which good Germans should shun. Smoking, too, was held to be unsuitable; citizens were urged to tell women they saw with a cigarette in public that it did not improve their image as mothers of the young.

An interesting detail is that despite the restrictive Nazi attitude in sexual matters, lesbians went largely untroubled. Following the murder of Röhm in 1934, scandalous reports came out about what were described as his 'perversions'. This led to police hunts and prosecutions under the laws against homosexual practices. During the Nazi period, 50,000 men were convicted of 'indecency'; of these some 15,000 were put in concentration camps. Yet, despite females being equally liable under the law, there was not a single case of a lesbian being charged. The authorities seemed to prefer to rely on the various female organizations to educate women into respectable behaviour. The NSF did its part in this by running a campaign against 'masculinization', by which was meant the tendency in women's fashions and hair-styling 'to blur the differences between the sexes'. It also tried to impress women with the fact that what the beloved *Führer* admired in German women was their 'feminine grace and female charm'. It is always difficult to measure precisely the influence of such campaigns. What can be said is that in all societies most people have a wish to be socially acceptable. The amount of coercion from the top did not have to be that heavy in Germany for people to be willing, even enthusiastic, to co-operate with the authorities' attempts to establish high social standards. It was part of that German conservatism of which Hitler was always very conscious.

Education

An area where policy towards women could be applied more formally was education. The school curriculum for girls was based on the understanding that few of them would go on to university. School staff were to teach with that in mind and not waste time on unnecessary intellectual training. Crafts and skills that would make the girls good home-makers were encouraged. It was recognized that there would always be a need for educated women as nurses and teachers but these were specialist areas of training, which were of no relevance to the majority of the girls.

How limiting this could be is evident from the following timetable from a standard secondary girl's school.

	Monday	Tuesday	Wednesday	Thursday	Friday	Saturday
8.00	German	German	German	German	German	German
8.50	Geography	History	Singing	Geography	History	Singing
9.40	Race Study	Race Study	Race Study	Ideology	Ideology	Ideology
10.25	Break	Break	Break	Break	Break	
11.00	Domestic Science	Domestic Science	Domestic Science	Domestic Science	Domestic Science	
12.10	Eugenics and Health	Eugenics and Health	Eugenics and Health	Eugenics and Health	Eugenics and Health	

The heavy emphasis on race and ideology points to the use of the schools as a major means of inculcating Nazi racial theories. There seems to have been little sustained protest over this from the staff. Teaches' careers could be blighted, perhaps ended, if they spoke out. Progressively through the 1930s, as happened in the legal and medical professions, Jews were demoted from responsible positions and then dismissed altogether.

As the textbooks used indicated, the race theories the girls studied were of a simple, repetitive, 'Aryans good – Jews bad' kind. History was presented as a study of the Jews trying to undermine the great achievements of the Germans. This was backed in the eugenics classes by models which showed that, as in nature, harmful germs could corrupt the whole body, so, in society, the Jews could damage the whole people.

The League of German Maidens

Outside school hours, girls were encouraged to join the League of German Maidens (*BDM* in its German initials). This was the sister movement to the boys' Hitler Youth. Both were Nazi organizations aimed at providing an outdoor life that would keep the young people healthy at the same time as it developed their understanding of National Socialism and made them feel truly part of the *Volk* (literally, 'the people' but it also conveys the sense of the community of Germans). The BDM was the girl guides with politics added. Its essential purpose was explained by Jutta Rudinger, one the BDM's national leaders. She spoke of what the movement would bring out in the girls: 'character and the ability to perform, not useless knowledge, but an all-round education, and an exemplary bearing.'

The great attraction for most of the girls was that the BDM got them out of the house and away from their parents, often for lengthy periods of time as when on camp. Renata Finkh, who had been a BDM member, later reflected on its attraction for her:

> I needed a group outside my parents' house, since there was nobody at home who really had any time for me. True, I also felt like an outsider even in the BDM, but slogans like '*Jungmädel* ['young woman'], the *Führer* needs you too!' affected me deeply. To be actually needed for a higher goal filled me with happiness and pride.

The obvious aim of the Nazi bosses in creating a youth movement was to produce political conformity in the young so that they would go on as adults to have unquestioning loyalty to National Socialism. But it is also important to appreciate that, for all its politics, the BDM did give young women, like Renata Finkh, a sense of pride and self-worth which they are unlikely to have got from anything else. It also introduced them to people of their own age from other classes and regions of Germany whom they would never have met but for the BDM.

At first, membership of both the Hitler Youth and the BDM was voluntary, but there was strong peer pressure on the young to join. This may in part explain the movement's popularity in the 1930s. Taken together, they showed an increase in membership from 108,000 in 1932 to 7.3 million in 1939. These numbers included the 10–14 years-olds who belonged to the DJ and the JM, younger versions (equivalent to the cubs and brownies) of the BDM and Hitler Youth. In 1939 membership was made compulsory, an indication both of the success of the movement and the tightening of central control in the Third Reich.

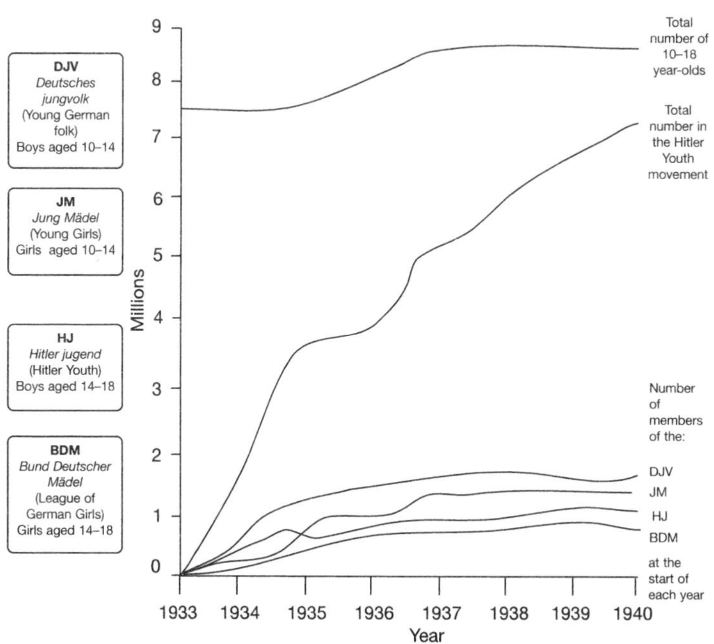

figure 14 graph showing membership of the various Nazi organizations for young people

It was also in 1939, at the outbreak of war in September, that another system was made compulsory for young woman. This was the Land Year Programme, a form of national service requiring unattached females to spend between six months and a year working on farms. It was no easy life. The farm camps were usually military-style barracks with primitive washing and toilet facilities. The work could be unremittingly hard.

A typical day might go like this:

5.30 – rise	17.00 – household work
6.00 – work in the fields	18.00 – break
8.00 – breakfast	18.30 – recreation
8.30 – work in the fields	19.30 – political instruction
12.00 – lunch	20.30 – supper
13.00 – political lecture	21.00 – singing
14.00 – sports drill	21.30 –lights out
16.00 – political class	

A diary entry kept by one the girls at a camp in Ruegen read:

> All is shit here. The toilets and showers are army-type and unpartitioned. The dormitories, two of them with fifty beds in each, contain nothing else, not even a chair. And they have no doors. Eva and Anita, standing in the doorways, order us to bed. And a command is the last thing we hear at night. 'Eyes closed! Everyone face the door!' We do. Who wants to stand barefoot on cold cement for an hour? Uschi and I already experienced 12 hours of this punishment for nothing worse than a giggle or a whisper.

The impact of the war

The coming of the war threw every social policy into the air. The priority for the organizers of young labour quickly changed to assisting the war effort. The training of young women was no longer about motherhood and domesticity but about sustaining the great military struggle. The pressure of war also obliged the Nazis to drop their opposition to women in the work force. Their attitude turned 180 degrees and they now began to encourage, even to demand, that women go into the factories. By the last full year of the war, over half the industrial workers in Germany were women.

	Germany	Britain
1939	37.3%	26.4%
1940	41.4%	29.8%
1941	42.6%	33.2%
1942	46.0%	35.1%
1943	48.8%	37.7%
1944	51.6%	37.9%

table 13 proportion of German women in the workforce (with Britain as a comparison) 1939–44

The war was a great destroyer in Germany and not simply in material terms. So desperate did the struggle become in its later stages that social convention gave way before it. The huge gaps that appeared in manpower as the lists of war dead lengthened could be filled in only one way. German women would have to produce children in such numbers that Germany's future could be secured. But the absence of men and the death of so many husbands meant that marriage as the normal source of regeneration was no longer physically possible. Himmler pointed the way. Since the traditional conventions governing the relations between the sexes had broken down, German women should gives themselves to men outside the normal confines of marriage.

> Beyond the bounds of perhaps otherwise necessary law and usage, and outside the sphere of marriage, it will be the sublime task of German women and girls of good blood, acting not frivolously but from a profound moral seriousness, to become mothers to children of soldiers setting off to battle, of whom destiny alone knows if they will return or die for Germany.
>
> (Himmler, 1944)

The Ministry of Justice supported Himmler's view. In 1944 it ruled that the leaders of German youth organizations were acting quite legally in urging the girls to have illegitimate children.

> The leaders have pointed out that in view of the prevailing shortage of men, not every girl could expect to get a husband in the future, and that the girls should at least fulfil their task as German women and donate a child to the *Führer*.

The reality was that the war had changed everything. The Nazis found that it was impossible to sustain their traditional policies towards women in the face of a war that threatened to, and ultimately did, destroy society.

Hitler's women

Heinrich Hoffmann, Hitler's official photographer and one of his few close companions, remarked of him:

> Very occasionally, a woman would be admitted to our intimate circle but she was never allowed to become the centre of it, and had to remain seen but not heard. She could, occasionally, take a small part in the conversation, but never allowed to hold forth or contradict Hitler.
>
> (Heinrich Hoffmann, *Hitler was my friend*, 1955)

That description is consistent with everything we know for certain about Hitler's relationships with women. With one exception, they were never central to his private life. The Nazi propaganda line was that since he was wedded to Germany he had no need to trouble himself with women or look for a wife. Yet there were two particular women who touched his life who deserve to be remembered for their own sake as well as for what they tell us about him and the system he created.

Angela 'Geli' Raubl (1908–31)

Geli Raubl died for Hitler's sake. When she became a student at Munich University in 1929, it was innocently arranged by her mother for Geli to stay with her 'Uncle Alf', as Hitler was known in the family. He found the pretty 21-year-old girl delightful company and soon became besotted by her. He loved to be seen out with her and showed her off to his friends. It is unlikely they had sexual relations; as far as is reliably known Hitler was asexual – he simply was not interested in that sort of thing. (A German scholar has suggested that he may have had undeveloped genitalia.)

He could nevertheless be intensely possessive and he was with Geli. He became bitterly and needlessly jealous of her. She had to dress according to his instructions and not go out unless he gave her permission. She was not allowed to socialize or to speak with people unless he vetted them first.

In 1931, Geli, lonely, oppressed and depressed, shot herself with his pistol. Her death caused a scandal in Munich and there were suggestions that she had been murdered. However, a police investigation found no evidence of this. Hitler, who had not been in Munich when she committed suicide, became hysterical when he learned of her death. He appeared devastated and inconsolable. But only for a time. Having paid one visit to her grave in Vienna, he suddenly decided to put the whole thing behind him and return to the political life that the scandal of her death had interrupted.

The fierce jealousy he showed towards Geli Raubl and the grief that briefly consumed him after she had killed herself offer an interesting insight into the inner Hitler. There was an emotional immaturity about him that stands in marked contrast to the powerful image that he gave as a public figure.

Eva Braun (1912–45)

Eva Braun is usually described in books as Hitler's mistress. A better term would be companion. Theirs was no grand passion. She served as his help mate but it was a one-sided affair. Eva had to be there when he needed her but she had no claim on his time or attention. She had no official position and was seldom present on formal occasions. The Nazi-dominated press seldom referred to her and it is probable that most Germans were unaware of her existence.

She and Hitler lived together in Munich from 1932 to 1936. Eva was a kept woman, provided with a villa and a chauffeured luxury car, but given no recognized status. Life seems not to have been much fun for her since on at least two occasions she tried to commit suicide, apparently an occupational hazard for Hitler's women. From 1936 on, she lived with him at the Berghof, his Bavarian retreat, as his unofficial hostess. Visitors were never told what her exact role was. Home movies show her as a mildly attractive young woman leading a fairly empty existence in beautiful but remote surroundings. She seems to have spent her days reading fashion magazines and watching romantic feature films.

Following his survival in the 1944 July Bomb Plot, she wrote to him, 'From our first meeting I swore to follow you anywhere – even unto death.' She was as good as her word, refusing to leave the Berlin bunker during the final weeks of the Third Reich. Hitler wrote that she was 'the woman who after many years of true friendship came of her own free will to this city, already almost besieged, to share my fate.'

The pair at last became man and wife in a formal marriage ceremony, the day before they honoured their suicide pact. On 30 April they both took poison before Hitler shot her and then himself.

A fitting epitaph was provide by Traudl Junge, another woman who showed touching dedication to Hitler. She had worked as one of his secretaries since 1942 and stayed with him in the bunker, although she managed to survive at the end. In her diary entry recording Hitler's death, she wrote: 'I'm angry with the dead *Führer*; he's left us in such a state of emptiness and helplessness! He's simply gone away, and with him the hypnotic compulsion under which we were living has gone too.'

the Nazi treatment of the Jews

This chapter will cover:

- Hitler's anti-Semitism
- Nazi persecution of the Jews 1933–42
- the Wannsee Protocol, 1942
- the Holocaust, 1942–5.

Hitler's attitude towards the Jews

Adolf Hitler had three abiding objects of hate – Jews, Communists and democracy – and, in his view they were all connected. His detestation of the Jews was pathological. He believed that the Aryan peoples, of whom the Germans were a major part, were a master race, and that the Jews were an inferior species. From this followed his conviction that the Jewish elements in society were necessarily corrupting. Anything Jewish was bound to be socially and culturally degrading. Hitler eagerly took up a long-standing anti-Semitic myth that there was a worldwide conspiracy of Jewish bankers plotting to destroy the international financial system as a first step to Jewish global domination. The 1914–18 war, according to this myth, had been part of the conspiracy.

Hitler and the Master Race

For a notion that was supposed to explain human society, Hitler's concept of the Master Race remained vague and undeveloped. It was in the end no more than a set of assertions about the supremacy of the Aryan, Nordic and Teutonic peoples. And even these groups were never clearly identified.

There is, of course, no scientific basis for the notion of one race being superior to another. Aryan supremacy was a meaningless concept. Indeed, there never was a separate, identifiable Aryan people. The Germans of the Third Reich, as with the vast majority of the world's ethnic groups, were hybrids. The idea of a Teutonic or Aryan or Nordic master race belongs to the world of fantasy.

However, one of the great betrayals of science in modern times was the willingness of anthropologists and medical researchers in Hitler's Germany to concoct false evidence to support the Nazis' irrational racial theories.

Hitler's view of Bolshevism

Hitler's hated Bolshevism (Communism) because he saw it as a direct product of international Jewry. Beginning with its Jewish founder, Karl Marx, Bolshevism had set out to corrupt the world politically, just as the Jews were corrupting it racially. For Hitler, the reason why Bolshevism had taken hold in Russia was that the majority race there were Slavs, who, like the Jews, were a sub-human species.

Hitler called the Slavs a 'rabbit people', fit only to reproduce, but incapable of organizing themselves socially or economically. That was why he admired Stalin for his savagery in turning such a degraded form of humanity into something resembling a nation. In *Mein Kampf*, Hitler claimed that it was Germany's providential mission to be the saviour of the Aryan race by destroying Jewry and seizing the Slav lands of the East. This was the goal National Socialism had set itself.

Hitler's view of democracy

Hitler was also convinced that democracy was a product of Semitism. That was why he believed it was such a weak political system. It was based on compromise and lack of purpose. If democracy were allowed to operate in Germany, it would prevent the nation achieving its destiny. Once in power, Hitler dismissed the whole democratic process. The *Führer* principle (absolute loyalty to the leader) demanded that all decisions taken by the leader be obeyed without question by the Party and the nation. He regarded the growth of democracy in Europe as the result of Jewish lies. People had been misled by false principles spread abroad by Jews who were aiming at the destruction of civilization itself.

It only remained for Hitler, once he was in power, to translate his ideas into practice. In regard to the Jews, the 12 years of Nazi rule are a story of applied hatred, climaxing in an attempt to destroy the whole race in Europe.

The persecution of the Jews in Germany, 1933–45

Immediately after the Nazi takeover in 1933, Goebbels and the notorious Jew-baiter, Julius Streicher, began to organize open violence against the Jews. Gangs of brownshirts physically attacked Jews on the streets and smashed their property. The year 1934 saw the introduction of a law which excluded Jews from the civil service and the professions. With occasional lulls in the vitriolic daily abuse of Jews, as for example at the time of the 1936 Olympics when the aim was not to upset foreign visitors, verbal and physical assaults on the Jews became commonplace. In the autumn of 1935 the Nuremberg Race Laws created a systematic programme of legal persecution.

The Nuremberg Race Laws, 1935

- Marriage between Jews and Germans forbidden
- 'Full' Jews deprived of German citizenship
- 'Full' Jews defined as those having three Jewish grandparents

There was some resistance. For example, groups of Jewish war veterans publicized the honourable role they had played in the 1914–18 struggle; handbills were distributed pointing out that 12,000 Jews had died fighting for the nation. But these protests were of little avail against the daily waves of propaganda depicting the Jews as enemies of the people and, therefore, unworthy of being classed as true Germans. In the autumn of 1938 some 18,000 Polish Jews resident in Germany were forcibly expelled. This proved the prelude to the most openly violent action yet.

On the pretext that a Jew had assassinated a German diplomat in Paris, the Nazis unleashed what became known as *Kristallnacht*. On the night of 9–10 November over 100 Jews were killed in a series of violent attacks. The glass in the title was a reference to the broken windows in the smashed homes, looted shops and desecrated synagogues. As many as 20,000 Jews were rounded up. Blaming the disturbances on the Jews themselves, the authorities arrested, imprisoned and then sent the greater number of them to concentration camps.

Julius Streicher (1885–1946)

Aggressive in appearance and vicious in character, Streicher became a Nazi early in the 1920s and was involved in the Munich putsch in 1923. A devoted admirer of Hitler, his major contribution to Nazism was as the fanatically anti-Semitic editor of the Party newspaper, *Der Stürmer* ('the batterer'),which poured out a constant stream of obscene lies and propaganda against the Jews. He was hanged at Nuremberg in 1946.

By the time Germany was at war with Britain a year later in 1939, Jewish businesses had been forbidden to operate, Jewish doctors had been debarred from medical practice, and Jewish children had been dismissed from state schools. A strict curfew was imposed on Jews living in towns and cities. The war had the effect of intensifying the anti-Jewish outrages. With the occupation of Eastern Europe by Hitler's armies, it was now the turn of non-German Jews to be persecuted. Round-ups, deportations, and killings became more organized and more widespread. Concentration camps spread across the whole of occupied Europe. Special SS units followed the German army as it marched into Russia, and murdered thousands of Jews.

A truly horrific part of the story was the readiness, indeed the enthusiasm, of locals to betray their Jewish neighbours to the SS and to expose their hiding places. Late in 1941 further humiliation came with the order that all Jews were to wear the distinctive yellow star of David which by tradition was a revered sign pointing to the historical link of modern Jews to the biblical King David. However, it was now deliberately picked on by the Nazis as a badge denoting that the wearers were members of an inferior race which had to be identified, isolated and destroyed so that all good Germans could avoid being contaminated by them. 'We must destroy the Jews wherever we find them.'

The Holocaust

Originally the term 'Holocaust' was used in a religious sense to mean a great sacrifice 'consumed in fire'. This powerful imagery has led to the word being applied to the Nazi attempt to wipe out the Jewish race.

A key moment may be said to have set the Holocaust in motion. In preparing for war in 1939, Hitler insisted that if conflict came it would be of the Jews own making. This gave him the excuse to claim that war would offer the German people the chance to exact revenge for the Jews' leading the nation to defeat in 1918. He declared, 'The Jews have not brought about the 9 November 1918 for nothing. This day will be avenged.' He spelt out to the Reichstag what form that vengeance would take:

> I want today to be a prophet; if international finance Jewry inside and outside Europe should succeed in plunging the nations once more into a world war, the result will be not the Bolshevization of the earth and thereby the victory of Jewry but the annihilation of the Jewish race in Europe.
>
> (Hitler, January 1939)

Hitler's statement meant that once the war had begun, the fate of the Jews in Nazi hands was sealed. In 1941, Joseph Goebbels left no doubt that the *Führer*'s words presaged the annihilation of the Jews:

> The Jews wanted their war, and now they have it. What is now coming true is the *Führer*'s prophecy of 30th January 1939 when he said that if international Finance Jewry once more succeeded in driving the peoples into a world war, the result would be the destruction of the Jewish race in Europe. We are now witnessing the fulfilment of that prophecy, and a destiny is being realized which is harsh but more than deserved. Feelings of sympathy or pity are entirely inappropriate. Jewry according to its law, 'and eye for an eye, a tooth for a tooth', is now perishing.
>
> (Joseph Goebbels, *Das Reich*, 16 November 1941)

The Final Solution

Goebbels's words were the cue for the Nazis to turn Hitler's terrifying prophesy into reality. At the end of the war it proved extremely difficult to obtain from the captured Nazis a clear admission that 'the final solution' of the Jewish problem had ever been formally adopted as official policy. However, the Nazi leaders' commitment to the destruction of the Jews is evident from a number of documents, one of the most striking being the Wannsee Protocol.

In January 1942, confident that Germany was on the verge of a victory that would give it total control of Europe, the most prominent of the Nazi leaders gathered in conference at Wannsee, a suburb of Berlin. The minutes of their discussions reveal that the main topic for consideration was the 'Final Solution'. Reinhard Heydrich, who along with Adolf Eichmann appear to have been the chief spokesmen, left no doubt as to what the Nazi objectives were. In the Protocol recording his words, Heydrich identified 11 million Jews inhabiting Europe. He subdivided this total into regions: 131,000 in Germany, five million in Russia, three million in the Ukraine, two-and-a-quarter million in Poland, three-quarters of a million in France, and one-third of a million in Britain.

Heydrich's 'solution' took the following form: Europe from East to West was to be 'cleansed' of all its Jews. In a planned and controlled operation these were to be transported to Eastern Europe where they would be made to work until they dropped dead from exhaustion and hunger. Those tough Jews who might survive all this would then be systematically exterminated lest they form 'the germ cell' of a Jewish recovery. It is worth quoting Heydrich's exact words:

> In the course of the final solution of the Jewish question, 11 million Jews are involved. Under appropriate control these are to be brought to the East for employment. In large labour gangs, with the sexes strictly segregated, they are to be employed in these areas for road construction, in which task undoubtedly a majority will disappear from natural diminution. The evacuated Jews will at first be conveyed in trainloads to transit ghettos from where they will be further transported to the East. The remnant that is able to survive all this must be regarded as the germ cell of a new Jewish development and therefore destroyed. In the course of the final solution, Europe is to be combed for Jews from West to East.
>
> (Reinhard Heydrich, The Wannsee Protocol, 20 January 1942)

At his trial in Israel 20 years later, Adolf Eichmann admitted that all those present at Wannsee had agreed in general principle and none had raised serious moral objections to the 'final solution'. The only disagreements were over the timing and pace of the programme. Robert Ley, the Director of the German Labour Front told an audience of industrialists in May 1942, 'It is not enough to isolate the Jewish enemy of mankind, the Jews have got to be exterminated.'

Within months of the Wannsee Conference, special concentration camps were set up to carry out mass extermination. Among the most notorious of these were Auschwitz, Majdenek, Sobibor and Treblinka. As appalling as the butchery itself was the methodical way in which it was carried out. The whole process from collecting the prisoners, killing them and then disposing of their bodies became an industrial exercise, a matter of applied logistics. Bureaucrats sat in offices calculating how they could most efficiently destroy a whole race of people.

Various methods of killing were tried. The simplest was the shooting of kneeling prisoners who fell forward into mass pits which were then filled in. A more sophisticated development was the gassing of prisoners followed by the burning of their bodies.

For the exterminators the largest problem was not the killing but how to get rid of the bodies. The killing was relatively easy since most Jews went unresisting to their death, often not knowing until the last moments that they were to be killed. One standard trick, successfully and repeatedly used by the guards, was to tell the victims that they were entering large shower rooms to be de-loused or disinfected; hence the need to strip and leave their clothes and belongings outside. It was only when the taps and showerheads let out not water but gas that the victims realized their fate. It was then that panic broke out, but it was a futile panic. Once the doors of the washroom had closed there was no escape.

The scene when the doors were opened after the last victims had died was painted in hell. Mounds of bodies were packed together in a scrum of death, some continuing to twitch in a hideous dance. Children still lay in their mother's arms, cradled in a last vain act of maternal protection. The bodies were befouled by urine and excrement which the dying in their final terror had involuntarily expelled. But the stench was the stench of death.

It was then that the *Sonderkomandos* began their fearsome task of clearing away the bodies. The *Sonderkomandos* were Jewish prisoners who, in return for privileges, volunteered to be death's attendants. A piece of satanic psychology understood and used by the guards was that groups of Jews about to be killed would be far readier to believe that they were simply going to be showered if they were assured so by their own kind. The *Sonderkomandos*, therefore, before ushering the victims into the chambers, calmed them by telling them that there was nothing to be frightened of, that they were merely going to be washed. It was an example of Jew being made to betray Jew.

Some managed to survive the camps' horrors and cheat death but the great majority of those who did were then left with a deep sense of guilt. Why had they survived when their companions had been destroyed? The answer was often too fearful to contemplate.

Survival was achieved only by being totally selfish. Stealing scraps of food from fellow prisoners, gaining privileges, such as extra rations or a lighter work load, by co-operating with the guards to expose those who had broken camp rules. It was part of the dehumanizing process that the camp system deliberately aimed to achieve.

Alongside such understandable acts of selfishness, there were countless examples of heroism and self-sacrifice: mothers who shortened their own lives by giving up their own meagre rations so that their children might eat; men who took the place of sick companions in the work detail in order to offer them some chance of rest and so stave off death. There were even some cases of individuals who accepted death by pretending to be someone else so that that person, perhaps a father with children, might be saved.

But these acts of individual self-sacrifice have to be set against the great horror, a situation in which most people thought only of themselves and used the most desperate means they could to survive, even at the cost of betraying their fellows. The guards knew and boasted of the enormity of what they were doing. One said to a victim, 'The outside world just wouldn't believe it if we told them what we actually do to you scum.'

Some Jews accepted their lot stoically, taking comfort from their belief that as the chosen people of God they were born to suffering, and that it was their historical fate to suffer in this way the judgement of the Almighty.

What added to the appalling suffering of the death camps was the method of transporting the victims to them. In keeping with the Wannsee plan 'to comb the Jews from west to east', the transported were packed into cattle trucks for journeys that often lasted several days. Locked into wagons that had no windows and no sanitation, the occupants were given no food or water. When they reached their destination many had died; those who survived were in a desperate condition. They were then made to stand for hours while they were sorted into two main contingents: those fit enough for work, and those whose age or frailty marked them out for immediate extermination.

On average, two-thirds of each trainload were gassed within a matter of days. And even for those judged to be capable of work, the decision was only a delayed death sentence since the brutality, starvation and over-work to which they were subjected in the camps meant their lives were extended by a few months at most.

The extermination programme came as near to achievement as the circumstances of war permitted. In all, some 30 extermination camps, undertook the task of killing and disposing of thousands of Jews on a daily quota basis. Auschwitz alone accounted for nearly one million deaths, which was between one-fifth and one-sixth of all those Jews who were exterminated. Post-war calculations suggested that some five to six million Jews had perished. The worst period was summer to summer 1942–3 which saw the death of nearly three-quarters of all the Jews who were to be killed in the Holocaust.

Belgium	24,000
Czechoslovakia	276,000
Estonia	1,000
France	83,000
Germany	225,000
Greece	72,000
Holland	106,000
Hungary	300,000
Italy	8,000
Latvia	80,000
Lithuania	143,000
Luxembourg	1,000
Norway (and Denmark)	1,000
Poland	3,000,000
Romania	365,000
Soviet Union	1,500,000
Yugoslavia	70,000

table 14 Genocide in Europe – the Number of Jews killed in the Holocaust (to the nearest 1000) in Germany and the occupied territories

There was a decline in the number of exterminations during the last two years of the war, but this did not denote a lessening of the Nazi resolve to destroy the Jews. It was simply that with the tide of war turning against Germany, the extermination programme was disrupted. Indeed, one of the most horrific features of the Holocaust occurred during the last year of the war.

As the Allies pushed into German occupied territory on two fronts, a number of the camps were closed and the prisoners made by their guards to go on the most terrible of forced marches, whose sole purpose, since the march had no destination, was to make the prisoners suffer as much as possible before they dropped dead from exhaustion. Those who tried to escape were shot. A Jewish survivor of the forced march from Auschwitz in January 1945 recalled, 'It was as if they were shooting at stray dogs. They didn't care and shot in every direction, without any consideration. We saw the blood on the white snow and carried on walking.' The forced marches were the final great act of gratuitous cruelty perpetrated by the psychotics who ran the camps in the name of German civilization.

Adolf Eichmann (1906–62)

Of the many perpetrators of the Final Solution, one who stands out, both because of his involvement in the mass killings and because of his eventual fate, is Adolf Eichmann.

Like Hitler, Eichmann was an Austrian from Linz. He graduated from being a travelling salesman in vacuum cleaners to join the Nazi Party in 1932. After training as a guard at Dachau concentration camp he joined the Jewish affairs department of the SD. After spending some time in Palestine liaising with Arab representatives, he became an expert on ways of enforcing Jewish emigration and served as a chief organizer in Vienna and Prague.

In 1941, he was appointed head of the Gestapo unit responsible for handling 'the Jewish question'. At Wannsee, a year later, he was a chief contributor to the debate on how best to achieve the destruction of the Jewish race in occupied Europe. During the last three years of the war he devoted himself to supervising the operation of the final solution.

Although arrested by the Americans in 1945, he escaped and fled to Argentina. It was there that he was later arrested by Israeli agents and smuggled back to Jerusalem where he was executed in 1962 after a trial in which the horrific details of the Nazi extermination programme under him were revealed. He seemed such an ordinary individual that it was hard to think that he had perpetrated such unspeakable crimes. It was this that led Hannah Arendt, a Jewish writer, to refer to him memorably as an example of 'the banality of evil'.

Hitler's personal responsibility for the Holocaust

Hitler did not, of course, create anti-Semitism. It existed in Germany long before the Nazi movement developed and was to be found in nearly all countries in Europe. Hatred of the Jews was a strong tradition in the Eastern regions, Russia being especially notorious for its 'pogroms' – state organized attacks on Jewish people and property. Soviet Communism between 1917 and 1991 continued the Russian tradition of discriminating against the Jews.

Hitler's perverted genius was to turn the existing German anti-Semitism into a structured hatred that bound the German *Volk* together. So pervasive did resentment of the Jews become that it is correct to regard Nazi Germany as a racial state. It defined itself by its supposed racial purity and refused to tolerate any in its midst who did not satisfy its standards of ethnic worth.

There is no existing document bearing Hitler's signature specifically ordering the Final Solution. This has led some observers to suggest that it was not, therefore, his intention and that the Final Solution was introduced without his knowledge and perhaps against his wishes. This is difficult to reconcile with the record. Hitler's hatred of the Jews was a defining characteristic. From his earliest entry into politics, he had spewed out unremitting hatred against them. It did not need a specific order from him to establish that unrelenting anti-Semitism was one of his principal motivations. He did not adopt it merely for political effect. Useful though it was to him as a political instrument to cast the Jews as scapegoats, all the evidence suggests he genuinely believed what he said about them. That is why there is a terrible progression between his hate-filled reponse to the Jews he first saw in Vienna and the gas chambers of the extermination camps.

As leader of the nation, Hitler continually savaged the Jewish race portraying it as the ultimate moral evil. Occasionally, for reasons of diplomacy, he might appear to soften his line but that was purely a matter of expediency. As an official in Hessen remarked in 1936:

> The *Führer* had for outward appearance to ban individual actions against the Jews in consideration of foreign policy, but in reality was wholly in agreement that each individual should continue on his own initiative to fight against Jewry in the most rigorous and radical forms.

Moreover, in his speech to the Reichstag at the beginning of the war in Europe in September 1939, Hitler had declared that the conflict was the work of international Jewry which was thus bringing on itself its own destruction.

Two years later in his speech to the Reichstag declaring war on the USA he had blamed Roosevelt for what had happened. The President, he said, had become the pawn of the 'entire satanic insidiousness of world Jewry'. Hitler went on to repeat his earlier prophecy, asserting that as a direct result of creating a world war the Jewish international conspirators had set in motion a process that would climax with their total annihilation and that of all their race. This was not merely the rhetoric of war. It was consistent with everything that Hitler had ever said about the Jews. All that was needed was a plan and that came at the Wannsee conference.

Clearly, Hitler needed underlings to carry out his purpose. Perhaps some of the plans were initiated by others without his knowing, but much of what went on in Nazi Germany had that character. After 1933, Hitler seldom engaged in the direct work of government. When he was involved it was usually in giving the nod to ideas and plans that were put to him. He seemed to have little appetite for the mechanics of government. Yet his was the guiding influence. Nothing of which he disapproved could ever become policy in Nazi Germany.

An illuminating detail is that in January 1944, Himmler addressing 300 leaders of the armed services, told them that, even in the middle of a desperate war struggle, the *Führer* had urged him to give priority to 'the total solution of the Jewish question.' Himmler added 'this was ultimately a matter of a *Führer* order.' Himmler's speech notes read 'Racial struggle – Total solution. Don't let the avengers arise to take revenge on our children.'

Looking back, one can see the Holocaust, the attempt to wipe out the Jewish race in Europe, as the climax to a process that began with Hitler's coming to power in 1933. Such was his violent aversion to Jews that it was grimly logical that once the Nazis were in control in Germany they would adopt savagely anti-Semitic policies. The development of these policies is easy to trace. There was a savage momentum of hatred to it all that led from persecution to extermination.

Among the dead were also gypsies, homosexuals and religious sects such as Jehovah's Witnesses, groups whose race, sexuality or beliefs made them undesirables in the Nazi state. There is also a case for including in the Holocaust those millions of Soviet prisoners of war who were executed or deliberately starved to death because they were Slavs and the representatives of Bolshevism.

The wider european responsibility

In Nazi-occupied Europe the guards who carried out the brutal policies against the Jews were not always Germans. The perpetrators were Poles, Ukrainians, Romanians, Frenchmen, Dutchmen, indeed any national who belonged to a country which had some anti-Semitic tradition within it. These perpetrators needed little encouragement from their Nazi masters. It has been suggested that the really important question is not why the German Nazis persecuted the Jews, but why did so many other peoples so eagerly seize upon the chance to destroy their own fellow nationals who happened to be Jewish?

The truth is that most nationals in all the occupied countries collaborated with the Germans. Without such co-operation, the Nazis could not have implemented their plans. In France, it was Frenchmen who gave the orders for the Jews to be arrested. It was Frenchmen who loaded them onto the trains that took them to the labour or death camps, kicking and beating those who resisted or were too slow.

Odette Churchill, a French woman who worked for British Intelligence, was arrested by the Gestapo and taken to the infamous Rennes prison in Paris where she was interrogated and tortured. She recorded that what almost broke her spirit was not the physical pain but the realization that her torturers were her own countrymen.

So repellent is much of the material which confronts historians when studying the Nazi period that they run the risk of allowing feeling to interfere with judgement. The horrific nature of the evidence is an affront to moral feelings. In Western tradition, historians are supposed to be analysts not moralists. According to this tradition they should regard Hitler with the same detachment as they would Caesar or Napoleon, the Nazi persecution of the Jews with the same objectivity as their oppression by the pharaohs. This, of course, is almost impossible to do. Historians are human beings as well as chroniclers; they cannot remain unmoved by events which still have a direct bearing on contemporary affairs and whose participants still survive.

13 the concentration camps

This chapter will cover:

- the purpose of the concentration camps
- their varying types
- how they were run
- how the Nazi regime dealt with the occupied territories.

The purpose of the concentration camps

The camps began as a logical and terrifying development of the Nazi aim of removing from society all those who, for reasons of race, politics, religion or sexual orientation, were regarded as unfit to live with ordinary Germans. This meant Jews and gypsies, Communists, Jehovah's Witnesses, and homosexuals; these were the main German victims to be found in the camps during the early period of the Third Reich. With the coming of the war, the camp system was rapidly spreading across occupied Europe. Many of the new camps were set up as slave labour and extermination centres.

Hitler's coming to power in January 1933 was the cue for the SA to cut loose. They rounded up their opponents and held them prisoner in a variety of places; underground cellars were the most convenient. The standard claim was that those arrested were being taken into 'protective custody', a formula that allowed the brownshirt gangs to pick up anyone they chose since no formal charges were issued. 'Protective custody' meant there was no limit to how long the arrested could be detained. Soon there were so many prisoners that it became necessary to establish large centres to hold them. This was the origin of the concentration camp system.

The camps were not all of one type and their character changed over the period of the Third Reich. Some were re-education centres, set up to house political dissidents or critics of the Nazi regime. The regime was severe and often brutal but there was some chance of the inmates surviving them and returning to ordinary society. Such camps were meant to terrify dissidents by showing what would happen to them if they spoke out against the Nazi system or tried to organize political resistance. They were a means of enforcing political correctness on the nation.

Early public attitudes towards the camps

One must not think of the whole population living in terror under a regime they hated. Objectors to Nazism were always a minority. Many Germans approved of such camps, believing that the Communists, pacifists and trouble-makers who were sent to them deserved their punishment. As one bystander said in Munich when he saw two of his neighbours arrested and bundled into a lorry after being caught handing out anti-Nazi leaflets: 'Serves them right. It'll do them good. They'll come back better for it.' Comments such as these represented the prevailing view.

It is unlikely, however, that ordinary Germans would have been so willing to accept the camps had they known what happened in them. The truth was the public saw only what the authorities allowed them to see. The camps that were shown in the cinema newsreels and that were open to visitors, including Red Cross representatives, were model camps, prisons where the accommodation, food and discipline conformed with civilized standards. The camps that were not open to view became hell holes.

Dachau, on the outskirts of Munich, was the first of the major camps to be opened in March 1933. While it does not have the death toll associated with other camps, it has earned itself a special place in the annals of horror, since it was at Dachau that the guards were systematically trained in the art of causing suffering. Their motto was 'tolerance is a sign of weakness'. Having learned how to inflict the greatest mental and physical agony on the prisoners, they were sent on to other camps to impart their hellish knowledge. Dachau was a finishing school in brutality.

The SS involvement in the camps

By May 1934, a year after the first camps had opened, some 80,000 prisoners were being held. It was around that time that, following the crushing of the SA in the Night of the Long Knives, the SS took over the running of the camps. Himmler, the SS chief, appointed Theodor Eicke to oversee the restructuring of the system, a position he held until his death in 1943. Eicke set up the special SS Death's Head unit from which the camp guards were recruited. They worked in conjunction with the Gestapo who were responsible for the arrest and movement of prisoners between camps.

Eicke drew up a detailed code by which the camps were to be operated. It was a study in applied terror. It listed how the prisoners were to be dehumanized by the loss of all personal possessions and the replacement of their name with a number. They were to wear distinctive stars on their uniform to denote their offences: yellow – Jews; pink – homosexuals; red – political prisoners; black – criminals.

Their food was to be minimal and they were to be flogged or put into solitary confinement for minor breaches of camp rules. Persistent offenders or those who refused to work were to be shot. No pity or sympathy was to be shown to the prisoners who were always to be treated as 'enemies of the state'. The guards themselves were to be ever ready 'to carry out even the hardest and most difficult orders without hesitation.'

Initially, with the closing of some of the SA camps the number of prisoners actually dropped, but as the Nazis tightened their grip on Germany the numbers began to rise again. Himmler was offended when a number of lawyers began to ask awkward questions about the high death rates reported in the camps. He used his influence with Hitler to have the camps put outside normal legal jurisdiction. This was a critical move since it meant there was now no outside control over how the camps were run. Those who operated them were answerable only to Eicke and through him to Himmler.

Types of camp

From the mid-1930s the camps and numbers in them grew considerably. This followed an important decision to develop the camps from being merely large prisons into organizations that could aid the economy. Where possible, the prisoners were to become forced labourers. With that in mind, many new camps were sited near industrial areas. A grim example of this was the creation of Mauthausen camp, near Linz in Austria. The site was chosen because of its closeness to the granite quarries which provided backbreaking work for the prisoners.

So great was the number of women prisoners that separate female camps were set up. The most notorious of these was Ravensbrück 80 km (50 miles) north of Berlin. Opened in 1939 with 6,000 inmates, by 1942 it held over 40,000. So appalling were the conditions there, that it has been calculated that of the 133,000 women sent to Ravensbrück during the six years it existed, only 41,000 survived.

Some concentration camps were either developed or specifically created to work prisoners to death and to carry out mass killings. Hitler had given an impetus to all this by his 'Commissar Order of 1941', which required that all captured

Soviet officers who were suspected of being commissars (political agents) were to be shot immediately. In two camps, Sachsenhausen and Buchenwald, Hitler's order led to the execution of 22,000 Soviet prisoners. It was also in Sachsenhausen, as well as in other camps, that certain barrack areas were sealed off and the Soviet prisoners kept in them without food until they starved to death.

It should be mentioned that the Stalags – the military POW camps, were not part of the SS camp system. They were run by the *Luftwaffe* who in the main kept to the Geneva Convention in their humane treatment of Allied prisoners, although this did not apply on the Eastern Front in regard to Russian POWs. There were, however, occasional atrocities in the Stalags. Hitler, enraged by what is known to film-goers as 'the Great Escape' in March 1944, ordered that 50 of the recaptured escapers were to be summarily shot. The Gestapo carried out the order, a war crime with which a number were charged at Nuremberg.

Medical experiments in the camps

In a number of camps, most notoriously Auschwitz, the SS provided facilities for German doctors to conduct medical experiments on the prisoners. A major figure in this was Josef Mengele, the chief medical officer at Auschwitz. His special interest was in the characteristics of heredity. He experimented on sets of twins, subjecting them to bone, skin and tissue grafts. He deliberately cut their flesh in order to measure comparative healing times. He even tried to create Siamese twins by stitching two gypsy boys together in the hope that their bodies would fuse. Prisoners were also injected with a variety of experimental substances, usually lethal in their effect. His laboratory was full of the body parts of disabled prisoners who had been killed on his orders as soon as they arrived at Auschwitz. The spotless white lab coat that he always wore earned him the nickname 'the angel of death'. Mengele escaped earthly retribution by fleeing to South America at the end of the war. He is thought to have died in Brazil in 1979.

Other experiments at Auschwitz and Dachau were carried out at the special request of the *Luftwaffe*. Prisoners were suspended in tanks of iced water as guinea pigs in tests aimed at providing information that might save the lives of *Luftwaffe* pilots who had to ditch into frozen seas. Other victims were placed in compression chambers to test the human body's

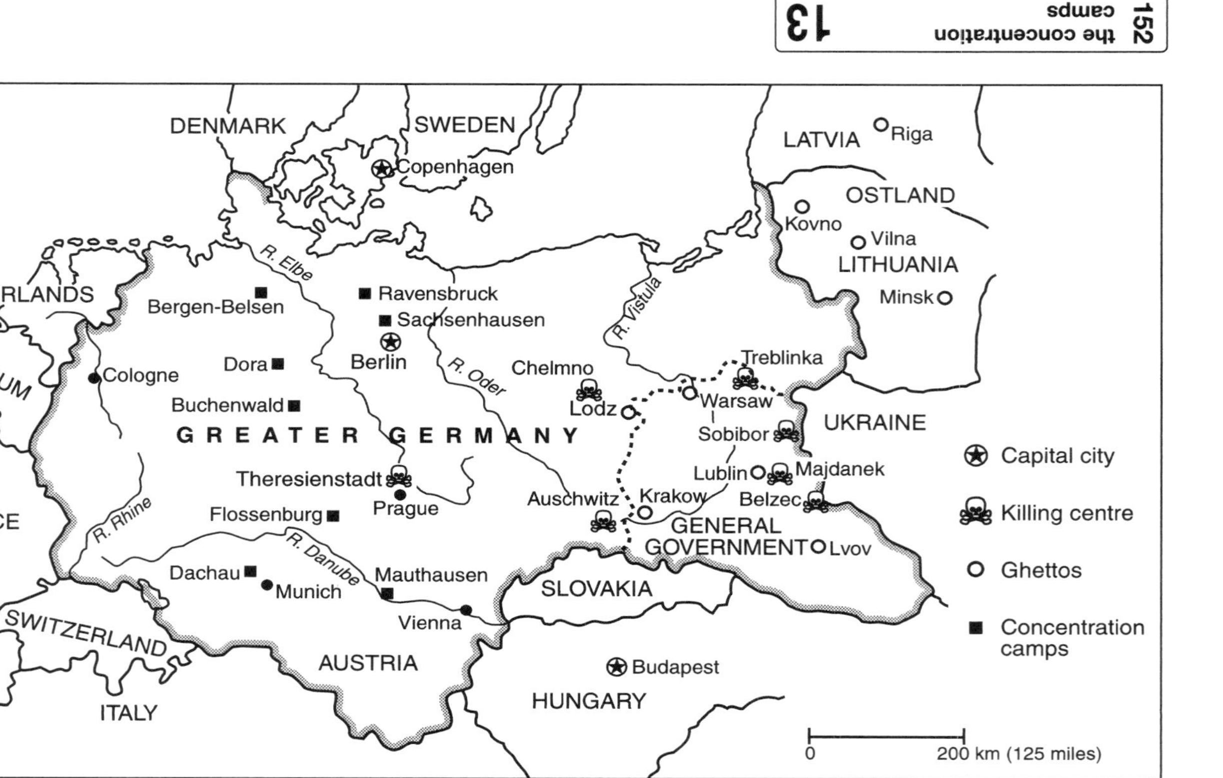

figure 15 map showing the main concentration camps in Germany and occupied Europe

reaction to extremes of atmospheric pressure. The films of such experiments were used in evidence at the Nuremberg hearings.

Auschwitz

Auschwitz in southern Poland, perhaps more than any other camp, has come to represent the unspeakable barbarism of the whole concentration camp system. But it would be wrong to think of it as a single camp. Auschwitz was more like an industrial city. Between 1940, when it was first established, and 1944 it grew to embrace not only Birkenau, a camp in its own right, but over 30 other smaller camps. Its position close to a large rubber and oil processing plant meant that its prisoners provided a constant supply of slave labourers. Auschwitz's size enabled it to fulfil all the functions of the system; it was a dehumanizing prison, a slave labour camp and an extermination centre. It became the great receiving centre for Jews deported from every part of occupied Europe.

Its purpose-built death chambers and crematoria became so efficient that in a single day they could gas and incinerate 6,000 prisoners. It was said that in 1944 a quarter of a million Hungarian Jews and gypsies were disposed of within one six-week period. In January 1945, as the Soviet armies closed in, Auschwitz's remaining inmates were forced to set out on a series of death marches while the SS did their best to destroy as much of the camp as they could. There will never be an absolutely agreed figure of the number slaughtered at Auschwitz, but informed calculations suggest between one and a quarter and one and a half million, of whom two-thirds were Jews.

Operation Reinhard, 1942–3

Under Operation Reinhard, three camps, Belzec, Treblinka and Sobibor, were specially designated for the destruction of the three million Jews of Poland. Directed by Odilo Globocnik, who took his orders directly from Himmler, the aim of the Operation was threefold: to organize the massive task of transporting the three million Jews to the camps, to exterminate and dispose of them after they had arrived, and to lay hold of their possessions for sending back to the Reich. Working with 450 specially chosen members of the SS who had perfected their skills in the euthanasia programme in Germany, Globocnik's team gassed as

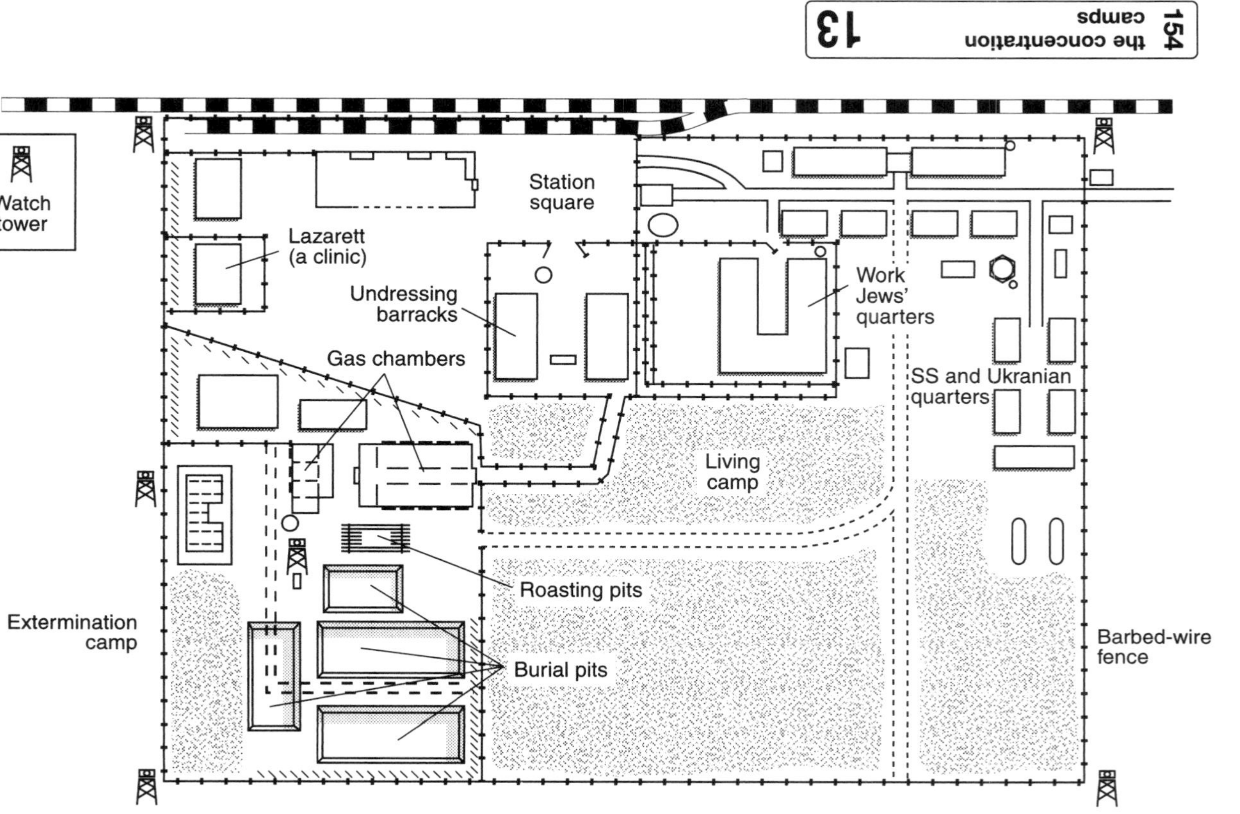

figure 16 plan of part of Treblinka camp

many as 1,500 victims a day. They were greatly helped in this by volunteers from among the Soviet POWs, many of whom were Ukrainians.

Operation Reinhard was a repellent success. If the death toll from Auschwitz, which was not technically part of the scheme, is included, over two and a quarter million Jews had been disposed of by the end of 1943, and their possessions, worth an estimated 180 million Reichmarks, had been purloined. Some of the money stuck to Globocnik's fingers, an offence that led to his demotion after the Operation was over. In May 1945, he committed suicide rather than allow himself to be captured by a British patrol.

Belsen

Belsen is an interesting example of the fact that not all the camps had the same purpose initially. It began as an internment camp for foreign Jews and foreign nationals caught in Germany after the war started. The intention was to exchange the internees for their counterparts held in countries at war with Germany. Conditions were reasonably comfortable at first, but as the war worsened for Germany sheer weight of numbers appeared to overwhelm the administrators of what was really two camps in one, since Belsen also incorporated the neighbouring camp of Bergen.

By default as much as by design, the situation quickly deteriorated. Food supplies dwindled leaving the 90,000 starving prisoners unable to fight the onset of typhus that decimated the camp. Josef Kramer, the dull-witted Commandant, who had worked in Auschwitz before being transferred to Belsen, had allowed chaos to develop. When British forces entered the camp in April 1945 they met with sights they could not believe. The skeletal bodies of 10,000 unburied dead were heaped in mounds around the camp. Another 40,000 lay in shallow mass graves. Of the 40,000 bewildered, emaciated prisoners who were still alive most were beyond saving. Within another month, 28,000 of them had died. Kramer was tried by a British military tribunal and executed in November 1945.

The impact of the war on the camps

As the fate of Belsen showed, the final stages of the war made the conditions for the camp prisoners more desperate than they had ever been. In an attempt to maintain Germany's factories, which were being blasted daily and nightly from the air, the decision was made to relocate as many of them as possible below ground. As a consequence the slave labourers were moved to underground camps where the foetid, airless conditions made it seem that they had truly entered hell. Aircraft were produced underground at Flossenberg camp. At Neuengamme, prisoners were moved into giant subterranean caves from which they were never allowed to surface. They had to eat and sleep by the machines at which they worked. When Hitler ordered that priority be given to the construction of his V weapons, Nordhausen in the Harz mountains became a nightmarish scene as prisoners were forced to live in tunnels burrowed into the hillsides.

Even the disintegration of the German war effort in the last months of the war brought the prisoners no respite. For many it was the worst time of all. As the camps were closed or abandoned, the guards, rather than release their prisoners, forced them to start out on what became a death march. It made no sense. Their was no purpose to the march other than to cause the maximum cruelty to prisoners already abused beyond endurance. The last official count taken by the SS of the numbers in the camps in January 1945 recorded 511,537 male prisoners and 202,674 female. Not including the Jews who died in the Final Solution and in Operation Reinhard, the number reckoned to have died in the camps is over 600,000.

Nazi policy in occupied Europe

The destructive momentum that the camp system had been gathering through the 1930s was quickened by the onset of war. Huge numbers of prisoners fell into German hands, especially after the invasion of Russia. Given Germany's growing need for industrial workers and the Nazi contempt for the *Untermenschen* ('sub-humans') of the eastern lands, tragedy beckoned. It came on a vast, barely imaginable scale. Millions of prisoners became slave labourers and millions were exterminated. Nor was this an accident of war. It was a meticulously planned and implemented programme.

The treatment of Poland

In the 1930s, Hitler had looked upon Poland with some favour. It was the first country he had made a treaty with. He approved of its aristocratic and authoritarian form of government and its strong anti-Semitism and anti-Bolshevism. The war in 1939 changed all that – Polish resistance had to be broken. This was not simply a racial matter; Poland's human and material resources would be of great value to Germany.

The Nazi-Soviet Pact of August 1939 gave Germany a free hand in western Poland to exploit the region as she wished. She did so with savagery. The cue was given by Ludolf von Alvensleven, Himmler's adjutant, who was put in charge of suppressing Polish resistance. Addressing the German forces in October 1939, Alvensleven declared:

> You are now the master race here. Nothing was yet built up through softness and weakness. That's why I expect, just as our *Führer* Adolf Hitler expects from you, that you are disciplined, but stand together hard as Krupp steel. Don't be soft, be merciless, and clear out everything that is not German and could hinder us in the work of construction.

On the pretext that ethnic Germans had been attacked by Poles, fierce reprisals were ordered. In November alone some 4,500 Poles were 'subjected to the sharpest measures', Alvensleven's euphemism for rounded up and shot. Such brutalities set the pattern for the treatment of Poland, which, following the German assault on Russia in June 1941, fell wholly under the control of the Third Reich.

Alvensleven's brutalities were built upon by Hans Frank, who was appointed Governor-General of German-occupied Poland in 1939, a post he held to the end of the war. On taking up his post, Frank, an associate of Hitler's since the 1920s, announced: 'Poland is a gigantic labour camp in which everything rests in the hands of the Germans.' He proceeded to administer the region with calculated ferocity.

Claiming that as the Master Race the Germans had the right to use Poland as they saw fit, he conducted a systematic rape of the country's resources and culture. The Polish economy was reduced to a bare subsistence level. Cities and urban areas were not to be rebuilt or developed. Educational institutions were closed as part of the plan to destroy the Polish intelligentsia.

Factories were shut down and their plant, removed to Germany. Frank decreed that all Polish property, whether Jewish or not, was subject to confiscation; many thousands of farms were seized and resettled by *Volkdeutsche* (ethnic Germans), who had been living in other parts of Eastern Europe.

Those Poles who had their land taken were then sent to Germany to work as slave labourers in the Reich. In addition to the 300,000 prisoners of war transported after 1939, there were over one million Poles working in Germany by 1942. Some of these were volunteers but the great majority were forced labourers.

This catalogue of exploitation and expropriation suggests that with the exception of parts of the Soviet Union, no occupied territory was treated so harshly as Poland. The German conquerors displayed a barbarity in keeping with Hitler's and Frank's concept of the Polish people as slaves of the Greater German Reich.

The labour conscription programme, April 1942

To sustain her massive war effort Germany needed a huge labour force. It was in order to tackle the critical manpower shortage that Fritz Sauckel, Hitler's Minister of Labour, introduced a massive conscription programme. It was to include all prisoners of war:

> A tremendous additional quantity of foreign labour must be found for the Reich. We must requisition skilled or unskilled male and female labour from the Soviet territories from the age of 15 upwards. In order to provide significant relief for the German housewife, especially for mothers with children, the *Führer* has also charged me to procure 400,000–500,000 strong and healthy girls from the Eastern territories.

As Labour Minister, Sauckel organized the deportation of five million people from the occupied territories to serve as slave workers. He ordered that they were to be mercilessly exploited so that they produced the most at the lowest cost. How far Sauckel was backed by headquarters was evident from this instruction from Martin Bormann, Chief Secretary to the *Führer* on 23 July 1942:

> The Slavs are to work for us. In so far as we don't need them, they may die. Therefore, vaccination and health services are superfluous. The fertility of the Slavs is undesirable. They may use contraceptives or practise abortion – the more the better. Education is dangerous. It is enough if they can count up to one hundred. Every educated person is a future enemy. As for food, they will not receive any more than is absolutely necessary. We are the masters. We come first.

Otto Brautigam – a dissident voice

In the excitement and self-congratulation, generated by three years of almost total military success between 1939 and 1942, there was little serious criticism among Germans of their country's progress. An important exception to this was Otto Brautigam, Deputy Leader of the Political Department of the Ministry for the Occupied East. He sent in a secret report in which he described how the brutal way in which Germany treated the occupied areas had destroyed a golden opportunity of gaining recruits for the Third Reich in its war against Stalin's Russia.

Brautigam made the telling point that when the German armies first swept into the western regions of the Soviet Union they had been greeted as liberators. The Soviet people, who had suffered two decades of oppression under Stalin, were ready to go over to Germany's side. What they wanted was 'liberation from Bolshevism.' If they had been treated with respect and sympathy they would have eagerly embraced the German cause. But instead they had been made slaves. The workers and peasants of the occupied areas had been despised by the German invaders as racial inferiors, fit only to be worked to death for the benefit of the Third Reich.

Brautigam said that the barbaric way the German armies treated their prisoners of war, together with the press-ganging of Soviet men and women into the labour force, ruined any hope of their becoming willing allies. Having allowed hundreds of thousands of prisoners to die 'like flies' through starvation and ill treatment, Germany was now in the absurd position of trying to recruit a labour force from the East. Brautigam believed that the 'limitless abuse of Slavic humanity' had united the Russians in a desperate struggle against Nazi Germany.

It is worth quoting Brautigam's words from 1942:

> The population greeted us with joy as liberators and placed themselves at our disposal. With unequalled presumption, we put aside all political knowledge and treat the peoples of the occupied Eastern territories as 'Second-Class Whites' to whom Providence has merely assigned the task of serving as slaves for Germany.
>
> It is no longer a secret from friend or foe that hundreds of thousands of Russian prisoners of war have died of hunger or cold in our camps like flies. Our policy has forced both Bolshevists and Russian nationalists into a common front against us.

The accuracy of Brautigam's analysis was borne out by the way the war developed on the Eastern Front. Germany's brutal treatment of the Soviet people led them to resist with a fierce tenacity that wore down the occupying forces. During two years of the most bitter warfare, from the defeat at Stalingrad in 1943 to the fall of Berlin in 1945, the German armies were to pay a terrible price for their earlier savageries. In pushing into eastern Germany in the closing stages of the war, the Red Army subjected the civilian population to the same ferocity which the Soviet people had suffered.

German resistance to Hitler

This chapter will cover:

- the resistance movement in Nazi Germany
- the attempts on Hitler's life
- the plotters
- why the resistance movement was unsuccessful.

The first bomb plot, 1939

On 9 November 1939, the German border police at Konstanz stopped a 36-year-old man from Swabia who was trying to cross into Switzerland. His papers were not fully in order, so they detained him while they made further enquiries. It was a lucky break for them. The man they held was George Elser. He had just tried to kill Adolph Hitler.

Elser was a loner. He had few friends and the people who did know him agreed later that he was an unlikely assassin. He appeared to have no great interest in politics, he seldom read newspapers, and he rarely attended political meetings. So what made this odd figure try to kill the *Führer*? He was inspired by a mixture of motives. In the early 1930s he had been attracted to the German Communist Party although he had not been very active as a member. Nonetheless, his sympathy for workers' rights led him to react angrily when the Nazis suppressed the German trade unions.

But it was something else – German expansionism – that led him to consider assassinating the Nazi leader. The Munich agreement of September 1938, in which Britain, France and Italy recognized German claims to the Sudetenland, the northern part of Czechoslovakia, was hailed by most Germans as a great diplomatic triumph. So, too, was the signing of the Nazi-Soviet Pact in August 1939, which appeared to guarantee Germany ten years of peace with the USSR. Elser, however, concluded that these successes would simply increase Hitler's lust for more territory to the point where the European powers would finally combine in a military struggle against him.

When Britain and France declared war on Germany after the invasion of Poland in September 1939, Elser's fears appeared to have been realized. He believed that once Hitler put his plans for attacking Britain and France into action there would be no preventing the descent into a European conflict in which Germany risked being destroyed. Even if defeat could be avoided, the war effort would demand unbearable sacrifices from the German people. To avoid such calamities, Elser decided that Hitler had to be stopped. Since the *Führer*'s power was unchallengeable, there was only one course of action left – he would have to be killed.

Elser had been preparing for this since the spring of 1939. As a carpenter and joiner by trade, he took a job in an arms factory in Munich. This gave him easy access to explosives and detonators. Over the summer months he smuggled out sticks of dynamite and timing devices. At home he then painstakingly assembled these into a bomb. To check that it would work he built a scaled-down model which he let off in his parents' garden. Knowing that Adolf Hitler often returned to Munich to attend party reunions in the Burgerbraukeller, the beer hall which had figured so prominently in the early days of the Nazi movement, Elser calculated that an opportunity for assassination would soon arise. Sure enough, in August he learned from newspaper reports that Hitler was to speak early in November at a rally in the beer hall to commemorate the Munich Putsch of 1923.

In the intervening period, Elser pursued a daring but simple scheme. For several nights a week he hid in the beer hall. After closing time he worked by torchlight or simply by touch, chipping away at a brick column to make a hole large enough to take a bomb. At the end of each session he replaced and sealed the outer bricks to avoid detection. He had chosen a particular pillar closest to where the speaker's podium was usually positioned. Two days before Hitler's visit, he placed the bomb in the pillar and set it to go off in 48 hours. He was so calm that he even went back the next day to listen at the pillar to make sure that the timer was ticking properly. It was. If Hitler kept to his schedule there was no way he could escape death.

The bomb went off exactly as planned. The timing device worked perfectly. At 9.20 p.m. on the evening of 8 November a fierce explosion tore through the Burgerbraukeller, killing eight people and severely injuring scores of others. Adolph Hitler was not one of them. Sadly for Elser, his planning had been too precise. Had the bomb gone off by as little as 15 minutes earlier there is little doubt that Hitler would have been blown up. But at the time of the explosion the *Führer* was on his way by car to Munich station. He had finished his speech and left the beer hall at 9.07 p.m. Not for the first time, nor the last, he had been extraordinarily lucky.

Hitler's original intention had been that, as usual, he would stay on for an hour or two after his speech, reminiscing with party members about the old times in Munich. However, news came from Berlin that important strategic decisions needed to be made immediately about Germany's intended attacks in Western Europe. This meant that Hitler would have to return to the capital earlier than originally scheduled. He decided to bring his speech forward by an hour and then forego his chat with the old comrades. It was this that saved him.

When the Party propagandists learned how close the *Führer* had come to being assassinated, they quickly turned it into a propaganda exercise. It was claimed that fate had preserved the *Führer* so that he could carry on his glorious work for the fatherland. Newspapers spoke of Hitler's escape as a 'miraculous salvation'. Nor was this mere propaganda. Hitler himself interpreted his survival, as he did all the other failed attempts on his life, as a clear sign that providence was on his side and would guide and protect him so that he could fulfil his destiny.

In the days following his arrest, Elser made a full confession. He was taken to Sachsenhausen concentration camp where he was treated as a special category prisoner entitled to a range of privileges. It was only as the war drew to its close that Elser was transferred to Dachau and then shot. The explanation for the surprising leniency initially shown him was that Hitler wanted Elser kept in reasonable shape so that he could be put on show trial when the war was over. Hitler's intention was to establish that the plot against him was the work of the British Secret Service who had simply used the deluded Elser to do their dirty work. It was important for public morale to convince the German people that the threats to the life of the *Führer* were not organized from within Germany. To be sure, some Germans might be implicated but these were isolated individuals in the pay of the nation's enemies. There was no popular movement against Hitler or the Nazi Party.

This was a propaganda line, but it remained substantially true throughout the war. There was no consistent, organized opposition movement in Hitler's Germany. When moves were made against him they were invariably desperate, doomed affairs, and they always coincided with a downturn in Germany's fortunes. When things were uncertain at the start of the war, and during the bad times for Germany after 1942, isolated cases of individual or group resistance did appear. But it is noticeable that between 1939 and 1942, when Hitler was making Germany master of Europe, opposition became dormant. What all this suggests is that opposition was rarely a matter of moral objection to Nazism. It was at its weakest when Germany was doing well under Hitler and at its strongest when his foreign wars appeared to be putting Germany at risk.

Resistance to Hitler

In all, there were to be some 15 attempts on Hitler's life. A number of Germans came to believe that only by removing him altogether could the nation be saved from defeat and humiliation. Yet not all resistance to Hitler took a violent form. There were those who genuinely wanted to be able to offer criticisms without being accused of challenging the system. The problem was that in the one-party state that Germany had become there were no legitimate avenues of protest. Criticism of Hitler or the authorities, even if moderate and intended to be constructive, was simply not acceptable.

This had one of two consequences: it either stifled protest altogether, people keeping their grumbles to themselves because of their fear of what would happen if they opened their mouths, or it led to desperate actions because there was no other way of expressing complaint. The second of the these responses required great bravery and, since the majority of people in Nazi Germany, as in any nation, are not heroes or heroines, it would always be a small minority who would be openly defiant.

The White Rose Group – protest by the young

In 1942, five students and one staff member at Munich University were drawn together by their dismay at the increasingly brutal Nazi regime in Germany and occupied Europe. The key players were a brother and sister, Hans and Sophie Scholl, who enlisted the help of Kurt Huber, a professor at the university, whose lectures had asked searching questions about the Nazi regime. They secretly produced and distributed a set of leaflets, entitled the White Rose (symbolic of peace), which called attention to the inhuman acts being committed in Germany's name.

It was a hazardous business, but they managed to avoid detection for over a year. It was the news of the disaster at Stalingrad that brought them into the open and led to their betrayal. Three of the group, including Hans Scholl, had fought as conscripts on the Eastern Front and so had direct knowledge of the terrors Hitler had led them into. Two weeks after the surrender at Stalingrad in January 1943, what proved to be the last of the White Rose leaflets carried this angry opening:

> Fellow Students! The nation is deeply shaken by the destruction of the men of Stalingrad. The genial strategy of the World War I corporal has senselessly and irresponsibly driven three hundred and thirty thousand German men to death. *Führer*, we thank you.
>
> (18 February 1943)

The group were making a last hopeless protest. They probably knew that intolerable language such as this would be the end for them; somebody would expose them. And so it proved. A university porter acted as Judas by naming the White Rose members and revealing where their primitive printing press was hidden. Within five weeks all six had been arrested, tried, and decapitated by guillotine. The university, staff and students, did not behave well. They praised the porter for his patriotic action and handed over to the Gestapo other students thought to have been associated with the six.

The fate of the White Rose illustrates the main weakness of all the opposition groups. Short of assassinating the Nazi leaders, which was so desperate a notion that it was usually rejected on practical, if not moral, grounds, there was little that could be done to organize effective opposition.

Of the different forms of resistance two main types stand out: the German left, made up of Communists and socialists, and the conservatives. The Gestapo described the left-wing resistance as *Rote Kapelle* ('Red Orchestra' or 'Organization') and the conservative as *Schwartz Kapelle* ('Black Orchestra' or 'Organization'). Interestingly, the main opposition to Hitler in Germany came from the political right rather than the left.

Opposition from the left (*Rote Kapelle*/Red Organization)

German Communists did not try to organize a broad resistance to Nazism within Germany. This is explained by the severity with which they were suppressed. Hitler was as savage in his hatred of the Communists as he was of the Jews. Beginning in 1933, some known Reds were rounded up and put in concentration camps. By 1935 what remained of the German Communist Party had been driven underground; it was suicidal for its members to offer an open challenge.

However, there was some easing of the anti-Red terror between the signing of the Nazi-Soviet Pact in August 1939 and the German attack on the USSR in June 1941. It was during this period that Communist infiltrators in various government departments had considerable success in smuggling secrets concerning Germany's military and economic strength back to the Soviet Union. But after the war with the Soviet Union had begun there was no chance for German Communists to organize resistance. Those who were not arrested remained quiet, intent simply on surviving.

A complaint made after the war was that the German working classes and the political left had been disappointingly reluctant to challenge Nazism. But this fails to appreciate just how restricted the workers were. After all, the independent trade unions had been destroyed and their place taken by Robert Ley's Labour Front which controlled the workforce under the equivalent of military discipline. Nor does it take into account the sacrifices that so many on the left were forced to make under Nazism. These are the figures:

Communists held in concentration camps by 1939 – 150,000

Workers imprisoned for political offences – 52,000

Workers executed for belonging to illegal organizations – 2,000

Workers who fled from Germany for political reasons – 40,000

Opposition from the right (*Schwartz Kapelle*/Black Organization)

By the term 'Black Organization' (*Schwartz Kapelle*), the Gestapo meant all those on the political right who were suspected of being anti-Hitler. It was never a specific body. Indeed, the critical feature of the Black Organization was how poorly organized and uncertain it was. Only in the loosest sense was it an organization at all, which had the odd result of making it difficult at times for the security forces to crack down on it effectively. The only point that united those included under the title was their feeling that Hitler's leadership was not good for Germany.

Among them were aristocratic and well-born Germans who represented the established elements of society. They were people whose distaste for the brutish aspects of Nazism was strong enough for them to wish for Hitler's removal. They regarded Hitler as a vulgar little man and they became disturbed when his war policies appeared to be taking Germany towards destruction.

Prominent among this type was General Beck, a Prussian officer of the old school, who was disgusted by the brutality that seemed to him to permeate every aspect of Nazism. He had resigned as Chief of the General Staff in protest against Germany's seizure of Czechoslovakia in 1939. He expressed his personal belief in this way: 'A soldier's duty of obedience ends as soon as he is given an order which is incompatible with his conscience.'

Another notable figure was Helmut von Moltke, a landed aristocrat whose ancestors had played an important part in the creation of the German nation in 1871. It was Moltke who founded the Kreisau Circle, a group that met on his estate at Kreisau to discuss developments in Germany. The Circle was wide; it included lawyers, artists, academics and trade unionists. Moltke did not directly press for Hitler's overthrow. His main concern was with preserving what was best in Germany so that it could remain a great nation after the war was over.

Those in the broader opposition regarded the Kreisau Circle as an odd mixture of idealists and pacifists. Stauffenberg, who was to be the pivotal figure in the major attempt to assassinate Hitler in July 1944, referred dismissively to the Circle as a 'little conspiracy-debating society'.

Not all German anti-Nazis accepted that assassination was morally permissible. For example, Dietrich Bonnhoeffer, a leading Protestant theologian, became involved with the conspirators because he was looking for ways of bringing about peace between Germany and Britain. He believed that this might require the political overthrow of Hitler, but he would not contemplate assassination.

Further assassination attempts

Elser's effort in 1939 was the first of 15 attempts or near-attempts to kill Hitler during the period of the Third Reich. Most of these were individual actions by people who never got close enough to their target to be a real danger. The more serious attempts always came from within the army. This was because it was among the military that the greatest dissatisfaction with Hitler was to be found, especially after the war began to go against Germany. There was also the simple fact that military personnel had closer access to the *Führer* than any other group of Germans.

In 1943 there were three separate plans to kill Hitler but all of them were called off at the last moment. In March, Major-General Tresckow put a primed bomb in the pocket of his new uniform that Hitler was to inspect. However, when Hitler did not follow his planned schedule, Tresckow just had time to abandon the would-be suicide bombing by defusing the device. He tried again, this time by planting a bomb on Hitler's plane. Again luck was on Hitler's side; there was no explosion. The cold air at altitude had fouled the detonator.

On another occasion, a conspirator planted a bomb in an exhibition hall that Hitler was visiting. Since it was judged that Hitler's tour would last at least half an hour, the timer was set for ten minutes after he entered. In fact, a plainly bored Hitler rushed through the exhibition and was outside again within five minutes. The bomb had to be defused in the men's lavatory.

Hitler's luck held again when Captain Alex Bussche volunteered, as Tresckow had, to die and take Hitler with him. Bussche planned to waylay Hitler while he was visiting a display of military uniforms, jump on him and pull the pin on a grenade. The day before the intended visit, however, the uniforms went up in smoke when the train bringing them to the exhibition hall was wrecked in an air raid.

The July Bomb Plot, 1944

Hitler, it seemed, had a charmed life. At this point the conspirators might well have lost heart completely. Indeed, they probably would have done so had it not been for Colonel Claus Von Stauffenberg. It was he who gave drive and a sense of purpose to the faltering anti-Hitler movement. Stauffenberg was brought into the circle of conspirators early in 1944.

Since the defeat at Stalingrad the previous year, Stauffenberg had become convinced that, as long as Hitler remained *Führer*, Germany was doomed. Hitler's refusal to acknowledge fully what had happened on the Eastern Front was proof that only by removing him could Germany be saved. Stauffenberg also claimed that the issue which finally determined him to act was his witnessing a mass execution by the SS of 40,000 Hungarian Jews, including large numbers of women and children.

Stauffenberg helped prepare a scheme whereby Hitler and other Nazi leaders would be killed, and the government taken over by generals and leading civilians anxious to end the war and make peace with the Allies. The plan was for Stauffenberg to assassinate Hitler at one of the regular military strategy meetings at the *Führer*'s headquarters in East Prussia. Stauffenberg was to carry a bomb in a brief-case into the meeting room, set the timer, and then, on the pretext of making an urgent phone call, leave the meeting.

That part of the plot worked. Shortly after Stauffenberg made his getaway, the bomb exploded. Hitler was thrown through the air by the blast which left him with scorched and shredded trousers, temporary deafness and an injured arm.

Two things had saved him. Because the usual venue, a concrete bunker, was being refitted, the meeting had been moved to a wooden hut above ground. This allowed the shock waves to spread through the splintering timber when the bomb exploded rather than being concentrated to deadly effect underground. The second factor that prevented his certain death was Stauffenberg's failure to carry out his original plan of placing a second explosive charge in his case.

Why were conspiracies against Hitler unsuccessful?

The failure of all the plots against Hitler indicates the near-impossibility of destroying a totalitarian system from inside. Hitler's shrewd decision to acquire and consolidate his power by legal, constitutional means had profound repercussions. It meant that any challenge to him was illegal; conspirators against him always had to act outside the law. This made them appear traitors in the eyes of the German people, who, though they may have lost faith in the *Führer* towards the end, rarely turned against him openly. Bound by their oath of loyalty to Hitler personally, the army generals were reduced to impotence. Unless they were prepared to break their code of honour, and few of them were, they could not move against their leader.

Nor were the conspirators helped by the Allies, who seldom took them seriously. Britain frequently declined to act on the approaches made by them. This was for two reasons. One was that by 1944, the British government was committed to a policy of forcing Germany to accept unconditional surrender. The removal of Hitler and his replacement with a more moderate leadership might well compromise that policy. The other was a fear, founded on previous experience, that approaches from apparent conspirators were in fact Gestapo plots to embarrass the British secret services and expose anti-Nazi Germans.

In the case of the July Plot, the most serious of the conspiracies, little planning had gone into the follow-up to the assassination. That was why when the news eventually reached the plotters that Hitler had survived, they panicked. When a shaken Hitler proved he was still alive by making a radio broadcast, the plot fell apart. Some conspirators committed suicide; others resigned themselves to their inevitable fate.

Stauffenberg was arrested and summarily shot. Arrests, torture and public trials soon followed. Freisler, the chief prosecutor, and one of the most repulsive of the individuals produced by the Nazi movement, delighted in humiliating the prisoners before him. These were show trials. The verdict was already fixed before proceedings opened. It was said that films were made of the hangings which Hitler then gloated over in private showings in his apartment. A little later, Rommel, who was implicated in the plot, was offered the chance to commit suicide to save bringing disgrace on himself and his family at a public trial. He accepted the offer.

There is a natural tendency to look sympathetically upon the plotters. Many of them showed remarkable bravery in opposing a regime which posterity continues to regard as odious. Yet it is worth remembering that not all had laudable motives; they were not all heroes. Some had been genuinely disturbed by the brutal methods by which the Nazis operated. Others were concerned primarily with saving Germany from defeat; their objection to Hitler was on national not moral grounds. Some were anxious to preserve their own position and status and judged that this could best be done by removing Hitler and coming to terms with the Western Allies.

The Churches

It would be reasonable to expect that, since Nazism in theory and practice raised so many moral questions and intruded on so many religious traditions, the Christian churches would have been foremost in resisting its excesses. There were certainly many cases of individual churchmen using their authority to question Nazi policies. An outstanding example was Dietrich Bonhoeffer, the Protestant theologian who attacked the Nazi militaristic cult and used his contacts with Britain to try to open peace talks. His opposition to Hitler and his work with the German resistance eventually led to his arrest after the July Bomb Plot, although he was not personally involved in the planned assassination. He was held in two concentration camps before being executed four weeks before the close of the war.

Another celebrated figure was Clemens Galen, the Catholic Archbishop of Munster, who was a constant thorn in Hitler's side. In sermons and writings, he condemned the Third Reich's racial laws, and denounced the abortion and sterilization programme as being contrary to the will of God. He described euthanasia as 'plain murder'. Although Himmler wanted him silenced, Hitler feared that removing him by force might provoke a major Catholic reaction. However, in the mass of arrests after the July Bomb Plot, Galen was picked up and spent the rest of the war in Sachsenhausen concentration camp.

Other brave clerics who deserve to be remembered were Martin Niemöller, Alfred Delp, Heinrich Gruber and Bernhard Lichtenberg.

Martin Niemöller was the Protestant pastor who set up the Confessional Church as a protest against the takeover of the Lutheran Church by the Nazis. On Hitler's personal orders, Niemöller was arrested in 1938 and spent seven years in concentration camps until the end of the war brought his release.

A Jesuit priest, Alfred Delp, joined Moltke's Kreisau Circle in order to help prepare the way for the end of Nazism and the introduction of a new moral order in Germany. He, too, was arrested in the wake of the July Bomb Plot and eventually hanged in February 1945.

Heinrich Gruber, the Protestant Dean of Berlin, made himself hated by the Nazis because of his sympathies for the Jews. He set up a number of organizations for the relief of persecuted

Jews, paying special attention to children and the elderly. Increasing interference from the Gestapo climaxed with his arrest and the closure of his Jewish havens. Despite being brutally treated in Dachau concentration camp, where a guard knocked out his teeth, he survived the war to become head of the Evangelical Church in East Berlin.

Bernhard Lichtenberg, a Jesuit priest, also took up the cause of the Jews. He denounced their persecution, one of the few priests to do so publicly. He went on to condemn the euthanasia programme and demanded that the Reich's Physician-in-Chief should be charged with the murder of the mentally disabled which, Lichtenberg said, 'will call forth the vengeance of the Lord on the German nation'. After two years' imprisonment in Berlin, he died in February 1943 on his way to Dachau.

There were hundreds of other lesser known clergy, whose willingness to risk their freedom and their lives in speaking out against Nazi barbarities remains an inspiring testament. In Dachau a special block was built for clergy who had fallen foul of the regime. In its time it held over 400 Catholic priests and 40 Protestant pastors.

Yet it has to be recorded that as formal institutions, neither the Catholic nor the Protestant Churches formally challenged or resisted the Nazi regime. On some big issues, of course, Church and State were in accord: for example, the desirability of an ordered, disciplined society and the need to fight against godless Communism.

This is a controversial area. One suggestion is that by appearing to co-operate with the regime, the Churches were able to maintain an influence on Nazi policies that led on many occasions to their being modified or withdrawn. Had the Churches chosen to condemn Nazism, as many, particularly outside Germany, said they should, it would have polarized the situation and made things impossible for those who were both believers and patriots. The question of what the proper stand was for the Churches to have taken in Nazi Germany is another of those dilemmas that faces people of good will in a totalitarian state.

The attitude of the Papacy towards Nazism has also become a matter of controversy. The key figure here was Pope Pius XII, who chose to take a very diplomatic stance. He declined to challenge the Third Reich openly and has been strongly criticized for not speaking out against the persecution of the

Jews. His defenders have responded by saying that he achieved far more through behind-the-scenes negotiation than by confrontation and that he let his detestation of Nazi immorality be known through diplomatic channels. It was also the case that he had special sympathy for prisoners and allowed the Vatican to be used as a haven for numbers of Italian Jews.

However, it also has to be noted that Church dignitaries in occupied areas often showed an eagerness to support the Nazi regime which went beyond mere diplomatic courtesies. When Hitler drove triumphantly into Austria in March 1938 to celebrate the *Anschluss*, the Cardinal Archbishop of Vienna, Theodor Innizer, arranged for cathedral bells to be rung and churches to be festooned with swastikas. The Cardinal also presented a joint letter from the Catholic bishops of Austria praising the takeover by Nazi Germany and thanking God that 'through the actions of the National Socialist Movement the danger of godless Bolshevism, which would destroy everything, would be fended off.'

Edelweiss

One set of German resisters with strong Catholic associations was the group of young people who took the Edelweiss flower as their badge. The flower, which grows in profusion in Bavaria in southern Germany, symbolized the group's wish to promote lasting German values in the face of the unnatural and amoral doctrines of Nazism. As an organization, Edelweiss spread to many parts of Germany. Worried by this development, the Gestapo, who claimed that a number of Hitler Youth sections had been infiltrated by the movement, was ferocious in hunting down Edelweiss members. In Cologne in 1944, 12 youngsters known to belong to Edelweiss were hanged in public. As with all the resistance movements, Edelweiss is remembered for the heroism of its members rather than for any influence it had on the German people.

Swingjugend (swinging youth)

A group that deserves honourable mention in the list of those who declined to accept Nazism is the *Swingjugend*. These were young people with a passion for American jazz. They were never formally a resistance movement and, indeed, made a point of being non-political – but they were social non-conformists. Their behaviour and appearance did not fit the Nazi image of clean-limbed, serious German youth. Their long hair, unconventional clothes, and taste for loud music led to them being described as 'deviants'. They were constantly harried by the authorities. A 'swing festival' in Hamburg in 1940, attended by hundreds of young people, was broken up by the police. The organizers were arrested. One of the appalling offences with which they were charged was having encouraged 'jitterbugging'.

Silly young people though many of them doubtless were, the irresponsibility of the *Swingjugend* stands in refreshing contrast to the dour and deadly seriousness of Nazism. In their odd little way the *Swingjugend* bore witness to the resilience of the human spirit.

15 Hitler and Nazi Germany

This chapter will cover:

- Hitler's last days
- Hitler's character
- German attitudes towards him.

The end

Hitler's last days were played out in his bunker below the Chancellery gardens in Berlin. It had the appearance of a badly designed film set for a Gothic horror movie.

Situated nine metres (30 feet) below ground the *Führer* bunker had four-metre (13 feet) thick concrete walls which kept out the sound of all but the largest explosions. Built in the mid-1930s and extended in 1943, it boasted 50 rooms serving official and private purposes. Enough food was stored to last for 50 days. There was champagne in abundance. The bunker was ventilated and lit by means of large generators that were petrol driven but could be hand-cranked in an emergency. Hitler had some three rooms for his own private use. It was there that he spent what were to be the last two weeks of his life. It was a strange, surreal existence. He continued to pore over maps giving orders for the disposition of armies that no longer existed.

Those generals who came to see him played the same game, pretending that they were still masters of their own fate rather than the impotent remnants of the once mighty *Wehrmacht*. Hitler's conversation became increasingly detached from reality. Outbursts of wild optimism alternated with savage denunciation of those who had allowed Germany to be betrayed into the hands of the Bolsheviks. He cursed the names of Himmler, Goering and Speer for letting him down. The German people deserved the fate that was coming to them; they had not lived up to the high National Socialist ideas that he had put before them. That he might bear some personal responsibility did not seem to enter his mind. As always, he blamed the Jews. He had now convinced himself that Churchill was Jewish; that was why Britain had rejected Germany's numerous peace offers since 1940. In the 'Testament' that he dictated during his last two days, he blamed Germany's plight on 'the universal poisoner of all peoples, international Jewry.'

Eventually, accepting there was no longer any hope and terrified of falling into the hands of the Russians, he and Eva Braun committed suicide on 30 April, the day after they had been through a formal ceremony that made them man and wife. They took poison after first trying it out on Blondi, Hitler's Alsation dog. It worked – Blondi keeled over and died. They then drank the poison themselves before Hitler shot Eva with a revolver and then himself. Their bodies were taken up to the Chancellery gardens and burned in a last act of loyalty to Hitler's orders. The Russians later came across the charred remains. The area where it all happened is now a Berlin municipal car park.

If tragedy lies in people being overtaken by a fate that they themselves have shaped, then those who died in the bunker with Hitler deserve, perhaps, to be regarded as tragic. It is, however, hard to feel compassion for those who died with Hitler. They chose to stay and die in a last gesture of perverted loyalty and defiance. It was perhaps a fitting end, that, still showing the same corrupted allegiance to a man and a regime that had long been discredited, they should have died by their own hand in a bunker that had become no more than a large squalid hole in the ground.

But there were innocent victims who engage our sympathy. Goebbels and his wife Magda in making their suicide pact agreed that they would take with them into death their six little children. Some time after being given sedatives to make them drowsy, the children had poison poured down their throats. When the oldest girl sleepily resisted, her jaws were forced open. The bodies of the five girls and one boy, aged between five and twelve who, only hours before, had been playing and laughing in the bunker corridors, were mute and terrifying witness to the monstrosity of a regime whose irrationalities had resulted in the deaths of innocent millions.

Hitler's leadership

Hitler was a lonely man. Goebbels, commenting on this aspect of his leader, once remarked that perhaps his dog Blondi was the *Führer*'s only true friend. Hitler himself claimed that his real friends were the German people. Yet it is hard not to think that he often regarded them with contempt. In *Mein Kampf* he spoke of how stupid and easily led the generality of Germans were. He shared with Goebbels the belief that propaganda could be used to convince the people of anything. At the end, rather than apologize for the disasters he had brought on the people, he laid blame on them. They were simply the rantings of a beaten, embittered man. He had never really trusted the people at any point in his life.

It is war that gives shape and definition to Nazi Germany. This is true in two senses: not simply in the obvious sense that it was the war from 1939–45 that took up half of the Third Reich's existence and put it to a test that it finally failed, but in another sense that, under Hitler, Germany was always at war. Hitler's language was the language of conflict. Everything was refracted through the prism of his warlike mind. He continually spoke of enemies: racial enemies, political enemies, international enemies, enemies within and enemies without, enemies to be destroyed without mercy.

Some of this was rhetoric, perhaps, said for effect. But all of it attunes with what we know of Hitler. He was a man of hate. Without hate he did not exist. Take away his hatred and you have drained him of his lifeblood.

For all the mixture of banality, prejudice and absurdity that made up Adolf Hitler, he was possessed of undoubted genius. He turned himself by sheer effort of will into a brilliant orator with a mesmerizing capacity to convince his listeners of the truth of his utterances. Nor was it merely on the grand scale that he operated. More than one general went to see him in the later stages of the war to explain that Germany's military position was hopeless and that the end was nigh, only for them to come out from the interview convinced that the nation could not lose.

Hitler was a parochial little man. He rarely travelled abroad, never staying anywhere outside Austria or Germany for longer than one day. The only exceptions were his enforced stays as a soldier on the Western Front and a brief period he spent in Italy as Mussolini's guest in 1941. Even his triumphal visit to Paris in 1940 was completed within a day.

Hitler's style of government

Everything that was done in Germany after 1933 was done in Hitler's name. It is difficult to accept that anything of which he really disapproved would have been pursued against his express command. He was the presiding genius. His was the ultimate responsibility.

Yet he was not a workaholic like Heinrich Himmler sitting at his working desk for 18 hours a day. A typical day for Hitler at the Berghof was for him to rise around midday, take lunch and then watch films in his private cinema. In the evening he would receive guests. It was then that he might speak to officials and ministers and give them his opinions on events of the day.

In that sense Hitler was rather like an absolute monarch of the early modern period, albeit a plebeian one. He did little himself, but nothing of importance could happen unless he willed it. The possible exception came with the running of the war. He liked to play the role of Commander-in-Chief, instructing his generals on strategy. One of the most extraordinary images in Nazi Germany is that of Lance Corporal Hitler laying down military law to the aristocratic generals of the high command who sometimes literally trembled in his presence.

It was an odd situation. Germany was certainly not a powerfully integrated political structure yet everything went through the *Führer*, even though, particularly after the war came, he was often remote, either in his Prussian headquarters or in the Berghof in southern Germany.

Hitler exercised his power in a strange way. After stripping the Reichstag of its powers and becoming both President and Chancellor of the Reich, there was no real constitutional limit to his authority. Yet he did not set about creating a whole new legal and governmental system. He left most of the institutions and the civil servants who ran them in place. When he wanted something particular doing, he would set up agencies or bodies with special powers and give them the right to act on their own jurisdiction. This was particularly true of economic policy.

As for the business of government, it was not something that especially interested him. He certainly did not engage in it on a daily basis. The average size of the entourage around Hitler was 35 people. These included secretaries, cooks, radio-operators and bodyguards. To these could be added at various times the visitors who might stay at his residences. He preferred to leave the work to the ministers he appointed. This gave them considerable personal power and room for initiative and led to often quite fierce rivalry between them.

The vital thing for any minister was to keep the confidence of the *Führer*. Those he trusted could approach him and ask for support for their proposals; as Chancellor any instructions he signed had priority over all other orders. That made the policies he backed unchallengeable.

Hitler's military errors

Hitler became Commander-in-Chief by default. Up to 1938 there was an official War Minister but when he resigned after becoming involved in a scandal involving a nude model, Hitler did not appoint a replacement. He simply took over the job himself. He commanded all three services but made no attempt to combine them. He kept them separate and seemed to encourage the rivalry between them. There were three commanders for each of the services but it was Hitler who made the big decisions.

He made himself so central to the strategic planning of the war that everything had to go through him. Churchill in Britain, Roosevelt in the United States and Stalin in Russia were involved in the grand designs but all of them gave precedence to the military. They might interfere occasionally, but they allowed the generals to run the war. Hitler did not. This left his generals frustrated. They knew he was making major errors yet they felt they could not stop him.

Had Hitler not had that awesome power his Third Reich might have avoided defeat in war. His mistakes proved to be of huge significance: failing to crush Britain when it was on the verge of collapse; ordering the invasion of Russia and thereby exposing Germany to a two-front war, which after 1914–18 all German generals agreed was impossible. These were among the most spectacular of his errors. Another was declaring war on the USA in December 1941 and thus involving Germany in war with the world's greatest military and economic power.

The list goes on. Having suffered defeat at Stalingrad he turned it into a disaster by not allowing a strategic retreat to take place on the Eastern Front, thus condemning millions of his troops to death or captivity. A smaller detail illustrates the stifling, destructive consequence of his authority. In June 1944 at the time of the landings in Normandy, the Allied forces might well have been pushed back into the sea if the German defenders had been allowed to call on the full backing of the panzer divisions. But the *Führer* refused to allow the tanks to be moved to where they were so desperately needed. The result of his stubbornness was that the Allies gained a foothold from which they began their inexorable push eastward into Germany.

In the end what drove him was fanaticism, a fanaticism which his generals, even though they well knew the consequences, declined to resist.

The German people and Hitler

In the end, Nazi Germany did not collapse because its people rose up and rejected the regime. That never happened. Nazism was broken by force of Allied arms, not internal resistance. It must not be overlooked just how popular Hitler was among Germans. His notions suited his times and the German people took to him as a saviour. As one journalist put it: 'Adolf Hitler – the living incarnation of the nation's yearning.'

In anything approaching normal circumstance, it is difficult to see how Hitler's fanaticism and prophetic utterances could ever have had much effect on a normal population. But post-war Germany was at a peculiar stage of history when moderation and decency took second place to extremism and aggression.

It is also too easy to forget that sometimes he was speaking sense. When, for example, he denounced the Versailles Treaty for not extending the right of self-determination to the German people, he was making a very valid point about the Allies' double standards in their treatment of Germany at the end of the First World War. Hitler's skill and that of his Propaganda Minister was in turning those legitimate grievances into a political programme of national regeneration that won over the majority of Germans.

Goebbels was working in fertile soil. The readiness of so many Germans to embrace Nazism made his propaganda task so much easier, a task which he defined as 'working on people until they have capitulated to us and united the nation behind the ideal of the National Revolution.' Nor was all this restricted to time-serving bureaucrats. Artists, musicians and writers were prominent among the declared supporters of the regime. In this sense the triumph of Hitler was a cultural revolution.

Certainly Nazi propaganda was powerful, but indoctrination was only one part of the story. The truth is that many officials kept their position by joining the Nazi cause. They saw that their chances of preferment, protection or promotion would be greatly enhanced by throwing in their lot with the Nazi Party. That is where the betrayals occurred. It was petty bureaucrats acting out of expediency that allowed Nazism to flourish.

This extended into the classroom and the lecture hall; teachers and academics were quick to join the Nazi side. In the year after Hitler became Chancellor, the Nazi Party grew from some two-and-a-half million to over four million. Nazism became all embracing; even apparently non-political groups like gardening clubs, choral societies and sports organizations chose to affiliate themselves to the Nazi Party. This was not coercion from the top, it was done willingly by ordinary respectable Germans, the pillars of their local community.

One of the most disturbing characteristics of all this is that those who might be regarded as the natural leaders of society – teachers, doctors, professors, priests and pastors – were among the strongest supporters of the regime. If they led, it was not surprising that most people followed. Germany lost its moral bearings.

The fact is that there has never been a more genuinely popular regime in modern European history. Resistance to the Nazis in power was minimal. It was only from 1942 on, after things began to go badly militarily, that opposition became significant. Nazism answered to the aspirations and needs of the great majority of German people. Tired of being humiliated, they took pride in a leader and a regime that elevated their nation's standing. Even if they understood little of the racial theories that raised Aryans to the status of a Master Race, they could take pride in national aspiration being achieved.

German guilt?

As long as the regime was successful it was supported by the great bulk of the people. Dissatisfaction with Nazism developed only after Germany began to suffer the military reverses after 1942.

But were the Germans, as an American scholar has controversially suggested, Hitler's willing executioners? Did they knowingly take part in or encourage the murder of Jews and dissidents? To suggest so seems a little harsh. Perhaps they *should* have known but they did not. Most of the SS excesses took place off camera. Until the last stages of the war it was possible to live in Germany without realizing the full barbarity of what went on in the concentration camps. It was only when the forced marches of the camp prisoners went through German towns and countryside in 1945 that Germans realized what was being done in their name.

Those ordinary Germans who were forced by the Allies to visit the camps after the liberation were genuinely appalled by what they saw. Again, perhaps they ought to have know what had been going on in these places, but they seemed sincere in protesting their ignorance.

Important, too, is the fact that the apparent lack of awareness was not restricted to the Germans. For example, many people in the occupied areas of Western Europe chose, for the sake of a quiet life, to co-operate with the occupiers; this often meant being involved in, or at least turning a blind eye to, the fearful treatment of the Jews in their country. That is why those who had collaborated were so harshly turned on, in France and Holland, for example, after the war. There was a deep sense of shame and guilt about what they had done.

It was also the case, extraordinary as it may seem to us now, that Hitler was regarded by the people not simply as a great leader but as a great man. He was the embodiment of moral virtue. The first line of a ditty sung daily in the primary schools went 'Mr Hitler is a godly man'. The accent was very much on his goodness. Hitler's was the name parents invoked to drive away the hobgoblins and bogeymen of their children's dreams. This may have been naive but it did express the esteemed place the *Führer* had in German thinking. A German psychologist wrote in 1942: 'The leader's charismatic power is not a mere phantasm – none can doubt that millions believe it.'

Of course, in the later stages of the war the bogeymen became very real. They were the Russians. A teenage girl's diary entry for September 1944 is revealing about the trust in Hitler that survived among many Germans even as things began to grow very dark:

> Rather sacrifice everything, absolutely everything, for victory, than for Bolshevism. What would I still go to school for if I am going to end up in Siberia? But if we all wanted to think in this way, there would be no help left. So, head high. Trust in our will and our leadership!!!

Seldom has trust been so misplaced or leadership used to such destructive ends.

glossary

Abwehr The army's intelligence and counter-espionage organization.

Anschluss The incorporation of Austria into the Third Reich which came about in 1938.

autarky National economic self-sufficiency.

Axis The union formed in 1936 between Germany and Italy and later joined by Japan.

***Blitzkrieg* (*lightning war*)** A combination of swiftly moving panzer (tank) attacks and dive-bombing by stuker aircraft, often behind enemy lines.

Bolshevism (Communism) The Marxist revolutionary movement which had taken power in Russia in 1917.

Comintern (Communist International) The Soviet organization, formed in 1919 and based in Moscow, to promote international Marxist revolution.

***Freikorps* (volunteer corps)** A loose organization of German soldiers returning from the war who still held strong nationalist feelings and who crushed attempted Communist risings.

Gestapo (Geheime Staatspolizei) The Third Reich's secret police organization.

ghetto A special enclosed area in which Jews were concentrated and not allowed to leave.

Horst Wessel A Nazi marching song taking its title from the name of the person who wrote the words.

Night of the Long Knives The episode in June 1934 when the SA was suppressed and its leaders executed.

***Kristallnacht* ('the night of glass')** The violent state-organized attack on Jewish people and property in November 1938.

the left those who favour progressive or revolutionary policies.

Länder The local state parliaments in Germany.

***lebensraum* ('living space')** The term relates to Hitler's notion of the right of the German people to occupy and settle in Eastern Europe.

Luftwaffe The German air force.

Nazis Members of the German National Socialist German Workers' Party (NSDAP).

panzers German tanks.

petite bourgeoisie The class made up typically of white-collar workers, shopkeepers, teachers, solicitors and minor civil servants who strongly supported the Nazis in their rise to power.

putsch An armed attempt to seize power.

the right Those who favour conservative or reactionary policies.

Reich Empire.

SA (*Sturmabteilungen*) The brownshirted storm troopers who served as Hitler's strong-armed men.

SD (*Sicherheitsdienst*) The intelligence service of the SS.

Sonderkomandos Jewish prisoners in the death camps who formed a special unit responsible for collecting the dead from the gas chambers and cremating them.

SS (*Schutz staffeln*) The 'protection squads' which under Himmler's direction developed into the vast apparatus of the state police.

swastika The crooked eight-armed cross which the Nazis adopted as the symbol for their movement.

T4 The organization responsible for the euthanasia and sterilization programmes.

Volk Techically it means the 'German people' – but it is a difficult idea to translate precisely. It refers to sense of solidarity and community that the people felt as members of the German nation.

Waffen SS The special military strike force of the SS.

Wehrmacht The German armed forces – army, navy and air force – though the term was often used to refer to the army separately.

taking it further

Nazi Germany is such a popular theme that books and articles continue to run off the presses in torrents. There are, for example, over 100 major biographies of Adolf Hitler still in print. The following is, therefore a very selective list of suggestions. All of them have useful bibliographies of their own.

An outstanding study of Nazi Germany, which is likely to lead the field for many years, is the two-volume biography by Ian Kershaw, *Hitler 1889–1936: Hubris* (Allen Lane, 1998) and *Hitler Nemesis: 1936–45* (Allen Lane, 2000). Another modern classic is Alan Bullock's comparative study of the two great adversaries, *Hitler and Stalin, Parallel Lives* (HarperCollins, 1991). A short but hugely readable biography is *Hitler* (Pan, 1980) by Norman Stone.

Robert S. Wistrich, *Who's Who in Nazi Germany* (Routledge, 2002) is a very useful reference book.

The medical details of the Nazi leaders, with many fascinating illustrations, were recorded by the American doctor at Nuremberg, John K. Lattimer, in *Hitler and the Nazi Leaders: A Unique Insight into Evil* (Ian Allan, 1999).

A short introduction, specially written for students, which manages to cover a wide range of themes is *Germany: The Third Reich 1933–45* by Geoff Layton (Hodder, 2000).

Antony Beevor's magnificent book, *Stalingrad* (Penguin, 2000) describes the pivotal battle that turned the war against Germany, while his equally powerful *Berlin the Downfall*

1945 (Penguin, 2002) details the last terrifying days of the Third Reich.

Michael Burleigh's, *Death and Deliverance: 'Euthanasia' in Germany 1900–1945* (CUP, 1994) charts the horrific development of the culture of death in Nazi Germany. The same author's *The Third Reich: A New History* (Pan, 2001) offers a fascinating interpretation of Nazism as a corrupted, secular religion. He also examined the theory and practice of Nazi racism in *The Racial State* (CUP, 1991).

A book which is both scholarly and enjoyable is Richard J. Evans's, *The Coming of the Third Reich* (Allen Lane, 2003) in which the author examines the Nazi seizure of power in Germany.

For an analysis of the many biographies of Hitler the key work is *The Hitler of History* (Alfred Knopf, 1997) by John Lukacs.

The mixture of courage, muddled-headedness, and desperation that made up the German resistance to Hitler is movingly described in *Plotting Hitler's Death: the German Resistance to Hitler 1933–45* (Weidenfeld & Nicolson, 1996) by Joachim Fest. This outstanding German historian, has also written *Hitler* (Penguin, 1977) and *The Face of the Third Reich* (Penguin, 1979), both of which come close to achieving the near impossible task of understanding what made the Nazi leaders think and behave the way they did. Fest's most recent study is his *Inside Hitler's Bunker: The Last Days of the Third Reich* (Macmillan, 2004).

Books which tackle the question of why Germans voted for the Nazis are *The Nazi Voter* (University of North Carolina, 1983) by T. Childers, and *The Nazi Seizure of Power: The Experience of a Single Town* (Eyre & Spottiswood, 1989) by W. S. Allen.

Hitler's Propaganda Machine by Ward Rutherford (Bison Books, 1978) has an impressive set of both black and white and coloured illustrations of the theme in its title.

Among the studies of the role and status of women in Hitler's Germany, two are especially recommended: Claudia Koonz, *Mothers in the Fatherland: Women, the family and Nazi Politics* (Methuen, 1987) and Matthew Stibbe, *Women in the Third Reich* (Arnold, 2003).

The Nazi attempt to exterminate the Jews is chillingly described in *The Holocaust* (Caxton Editions, 2002) by Aubrey Newman, a book that is illustrated throughout by haunting photographs and images.

A highly controversial book which argues that the majority of the German people supported the Holocaust is Daniel Goldhagen's *Hitler's Willing Executioners: Ordinary Germans and the Holocaust* (Little Brown, 1996). Goldhagen's views are examined in Ian Kershaw's *The Nazi Dictatorship: Problems & Perspectives of Interpretation* (Arnold, 2000), a book which though difficult in places is an excellent survey of the major debates that continue to rage over Nazi Germany.

Those readers looking for primary sources will find the richest and deepest mine in *Nazism 1919–1945: A Documentary Reader* by J. Noakes and G. Bridham (Exeter University, 1988).

index

teach yourself

the second world war

alan farmer

- Explore the events of the Second World War
- Discover its impact on those involved
- Understand the reasons behind the conflict and who was to blame

teach yourself the second world war is an accessible introduction to one of the most important, tragic and costly events in history. This war had an unimaginable impact on the entire world, causing the deaths of over 50 million people. Follow the main military campaigns of the war, discover how it affected the countries involved and develop your understanding of why the Allied powers were able to achieve victory.

Alan Farmer is Head of History at St Martin's College, Lancaster and has written a large number of books on modern American, European and British history.

teach yourself

the first world war

david evans

- Gain a better understanding of key events during the First World War
- Discover the reasons behind the conflict
- Gain an insight into the experiences of those involved

teach yourself the First World War is a compelling introduction to a conflict on a scale never experienced in the world before. When war broke out in 1914 some predicted that it would be 'over by Christmas', yet four years later, following the slaughter of over nine million men, still no peace had been made. This book considers the roles of the leading politicians and explores the impact on the civilians and societies involved.

David Evans is an established writer and lecturer. He has written over twenty books covering aspects of modern European history and is a contributor on both television and radio.